The Academic Chairperson's Handbook

A study funded by the Lilly Endowment, Inc., and
supported by TIAA-CREF

The Academic
Chairperson's Handbook

John W. Creswell
Daniel W. Wheeler
Alan T. Seagren
Nancy J. Egly
Kirk D. Beyer

University of Nebraska Press
Lincoln and London

√

Library of Congress Cataloging-in-Publication Data
The Academic chairperson's handbook / John W. Creswell . . . [et al.].
    p.   cm.
  Includes bibliographical references.
  ISBN 0-8032-1450-2 (alk. paper)
  1. Departmental chairmen (Universities)—United States.
2. Universities and colleges—United States—Departments.
I. Creswell, John W.
LB2341.A217   1990
378.1′11—dc20   90-30548
                                                      CIP

Second printing: 1990

916256

Acknowledgments

To the many individuals involved in the preparation of this book, we are deeply indebted. Especially we would like to credit Peggy Heim, Senior Education Projects Officer of TIAA-CREF, who gave generously of her time and provided continued support and insightful reviews of manuscripts. Howard Bowen of the Claremont Graduate School suggested the topic and encouraged us to proceed. Ralph Lundgren of the Lilly Endowment, Inc., saw the importance of funding the project, and provided encouragement along the way.

Two Advisory Panels, convened by Peggy Heim and TIAA-CREF, provided valuable direction in the planning and the review stages of this project. Panel members included Howard Bowen, Wilbert J. McKeachie, Claude Mathis, Shirley Clark, Larry Braskamp, John Bennett, Sang Lee, Jo Taylor, Allan Tucker, and John Ward. Other individuals - distinguished scholars in the field and department chairs and heads - provided helpful reviews at various phases of manuscript development: Walt Gmelch, Alan Bayer, John Braxton, George Antone, Robert G. Fuller, Roger Baldwin, Alan Lonsdale, Robert J. Stalcup, and Mary Megel.

We have pilot-tested material from this project in over a dozen regional and national workshops involving department chairs and faculty. Thus, we are indebted to the over 1000 people participating in these sessions who reviewed, reacted and responded to ideas and concepts.

Finally, this project is the product of individuals working on the "Lilly Project Team" at the University of Nebraska-Lincoln. In addition to the authors of this book they include technical writers, research assistants, faculty, and project staff: MaryBeth McWilliams, Patricia Murphy, Diane Greenlee, Marilyn Beyer, Phyllis Hasse, Luise Berner, Dona Beattie, LuAnn Kraeger, Myra Wilhite, Marilyn Grady, Ruth Wenzl Gerber, and Linda Vavrus.

CONTENTS

E very year, with little preparation, scores of faculty members across the country step into the position of chairing their department. Even in tranquil times, the ambiguity of being both faculty member and administrator - - not to mention scholar, teacher, advocate, counselor, and friend - - makes the assignment a tough one.

But these are hardly tranquil times. Most of the tasks routinely listed in the job description are becoming more demanding and complex. Consider what computers have done to equipment decisions, and what lawyers and litigation have done to promotion/tenure decisions. Or take the recruitment of new faculty. By one estimate, between 1990 and 2004, departments will need to recruit 335,000 new faculty . . . and do so in an intensely competitive seller's market, where the appointees want such benefits as suitable employment for their spouses. These issues raise complicated concerns for decision makers.

There's more. What we rarely see in the formal position descriptions are the *opportunities* department chairs have to provide leadership for improvement. Indeed, for most of the growing list of concerns and complaints about the "quality" of higher education, the department chairs are in a singular position to make things happen.

What if chairs took on the task of creating in their departments a new culture of professionalism about teaching? I'm thinking here of a culture in which faculty routinely shared their course syllabi for comment by their colleagues, routinely observed each other's classes, routinely discussed important "cases" of teaching like doctors during "grand rounds" discuss important cases of medicine? What if chairs committed themselves to designing methods of documenting and displaying exemplary teaching in their fields so that teaching could be genuinely peer reviewed?

To get all the way from here to there, I suspect that colleges and universities will have to lengthen the tenure of department chairs, and build more incentives into the position for department chairs to take this kind of leadership. Meanwhile, thankfully, there will always be chairs who - - in spite of the ambiguity, escalating demands, and lack of support - - want to do better now. That's where this book comes in.

Researchers in many professions are turning their attention to the "wisdom in practice" - - to what can be learned from those actually doing excellent work in the field. In that tradition, this handbook draws on the reflections of some two hundred chairs, identified as excellent by their own colleagues. Best of all, I think are the parts in which these chairs speak, in their own words, about the ups and downs of their jobs, and the approaches that have worked for them. Chairs now have a new voice. It deserves to be heard.

Russell Edgerton
President
American Association for Higher Education

Like steel bridges, academic departments are built with permanency in mind. As bridges span realms shaped by seas and storms, so also must departments span realms shaped by both the expected and unexpected needs and interests of faculty.

Whenen Joseph B. Strauss, a bridge builder of established reputation, presented San Francisco's City Engineer with the idea of building the Golden Gate Bridge, he knew that the bridge would be the challenge of his career (Black, 1933). No one had ever considered bridging a gap of more than 4,000 feet of water. No engineer had ever proposed putting a bridge pier into the calm water of the deep sea, much less in the choppy surface water of the Bay.

These were the known difficulties; unexpected difficulties soon developed. Objection arose from the citizens of San Francisco about the high costs of construction. The citizens rallied to support the funding only after their pride was challenged -- a new bridge was being built on the East Coast, the 3,500 foot George Washington Bridge over the Hudson. When Strauss built a steel trestle as a working platform out to the pier site, a 2,000-ton steamer collided with the new structure, causing delay. Next came the job of excavating rock beneath sixty-five to eighty-five feet of water. Strauss solved this problem by using submarine bombs to blast away the rock. The forms for pouring the concrete pier were constructed and placed, only to be destroyed by a sea storm, one of the worst in history to that time. The litany of difficulties is legend. Strauss overcame them by expertise, perseverance, and luck.

The building of a bridge provides a useful metaphor for academic departments and the role of department chairs. Just as proposals for new bridges find supporters and critics, so also do individuals criticize and acclaim the value of departments. While departments fragment and divide the faculty, they also provide a structure where faculty can interact with a minimum of misunderstanding and superfluous effort (Anderson, 1977). Like steel bridges, academic departments are built with permanency in mind. As bridges span realms shaped by seas and storms, so must departments span realms shaped by both the expected and unexpected needs and interests of faculty. Like Strauss with his vision for the Golden Gate Bridge, chairpersons and faculty hold a vision for their department. Difficulties arise in bringing that vision to a focus, building ownership of it and maintaining its vitality.

Academic departments represent a basic building block in the organizational structure of colleges. As the immediate workplace of faculty and staff, day-to-day activities dramatically shape individual attitudes, behaviors, and performances. Given the changing demographics of faculty, the diversity of individual interests and the increasing time demands on chairs, a conundrum today is building a department responsive to the professional needs and concerns of faculty.

This book, directed primarily toward academic chairs and their faculty, champions the importance of chairing (or heading) an academic department (or division) and focuses attention on the strategies "excellent" chairs use in building a positive work environment for faculty and releasing individual faculty potential. We base our framework for discussing this topic on perspectives drawn from human, organizational, and career development; systems theory; and interpersonal communications. We also rely heavily on recent research writings about faculty careers, faculty development, and academic leadership.

"Excellent" chairs are 200 individuals on 70 campuses who participated in our national study (see Appendix A for comments about the national study). Chief academic officers and faculty development specialists nominated these individuals for their excellence in promoting and enhancing the professional growth and development of faculty.

Some "excellent" chairs hold the title of "head" instead of "chair." In this book, we will use the terms "chair" and "chairperson" interchangeably. Both terms refer to individuals holding mid-level academic positions in a departments or comparable units. We will stay with the term "department" throughout the book, recognizing that the structural unit housing faculty may be called other names such as "division" or "colloquium." Rather than use the awkward "he or she" and "him and her" throughout the book, we will vary the gender of the pronoun, thereby giving approximately equal attention to the female and male voice. Finally, we employ the term "faculty professional development" in its broadest sense. Our meaning encompasses more than the traditional renewal activities such as sabbaticals, travel, and instructional improvement. It extends also to the personal needs of faculty. Thus, we concur with Kenneth Eble who suggested that chairs should be " keen observers of faculty needs and wants and . . . ingenious providers of motivation, support, and encouragement" (Eble, 1985, p. 2).

We present fifteen strategies offered by the "excellent" chairs and discuss their application in specific situations. Undoubtedly, the strategies reflect individual style, faculty issues and needs, and historic departmental and institutional values and traditions. This book highlights "good" practices of individuals singled out on campuses as "excellent" role models. By reporting the strategies of these individuals, we follow the lead of writers in the management and human resources fields who learned years ago that "excellent" leaders had much to share with colleagues holding similar positions.

We have attempted to preserve the original flavor and form of direct comments by chairs. These pages will reflect individual emotions of hope, frustration, anxiety, sadness, and surprise, as well as the regional colloquialisms of everyday speech. We report numerous strategies. You will need to select those that meet your needs and make you feel comfortable.

Strategies presented may confirm established approaches or present different perspectives. Although the examples cited are from other types of departments and institutions than your own, applying the strategies to your own situation can be a useful exercise. The strategies are upbeat, positive, and developmental. Our analysis, however, will not mask the sometimes harsh political realities involved in leading academic departments. Though "excellent" chairs discussed their struggles and frustrations, they did not dwell on the negative aspects of their jobs; they dealt with day-to-day setbacks in a resolute manner and kept a positive long-range attitude.

This book is organized in two parts. In Part I, we introduce several difficulties chairs encounter in building a positive work environment for promoting faculty growth and professional development. A self-assessment inventory at the end of Chapter One is followed by three chapters outlining 15 chair strategies. These strategies are organized around the themes of your own self-development, your role as an academic leader, and your interpersonal relations with faculty.

In Part II, we apply the strategies, first as a series of processes you might use in addressing specific faculty situations and second as a general guide for building a positive work environment. As you proceed through the processes for applying strategies -- helping newly-hired faculty become adjusted and oriented, improving the teaching performance of faculty, improving the scholarship of faculty, refocusing faculty efforts, and addressing personal issues -- bear in mind that the processes are a general formula for action, not a lock-step method to be rigidly applied in all cases. We end the book with a general guide for the departmental building process and present steps for building your department.

A synopsis of our national project on academic department chairpersons, our primary evidence for points made in this book, is found in Appendix A. Appendix B contains a topical index to the strategies.

Part I

Fifteen Strategies in
the Building Process

CHAPTER ONE

Difficulties in the Building Process

C reating or maintaining a positive work environment for faculty is a goal to which most chairs would aspire. This environment can be characterized in several ways. It is one in which faculty feel they are appreciated and helped. Faculty share a commitment to a particular unit. They support the chair's goals, aims, and departmental objectives. Undoubtedly, this may present a utopian prescription for reality, but it does represent a goal which most departments can achieve or at least move toward.

This chapter presents three realities that chairs face in building a positive environment: aspects related to chairing a department; characteristics of academic departments; and pressing problems facing faculty. The chapter ends with a self-assessment inventory that serves both as a means of identifying concerns and directing attention to relevant sections of this book.

Chairing a Department

Chairs are busy people. Daily, they face tough decisions about evaluating and recruiting faculty, providing raises, adjudicating conflicts, moderating tensions; and counseling faculty about diverse topics such as midlife crises, personal and professional growth, and early retirement. These responsibilities suggest a myriad of roles and tasks, well-documented in the literature on chairing a department.[1] Implicit within these roles and tasks are the dual responsibilities of loyalty and support to the institution and advocacy for staff in the department. A continual need exists to resolve tension on both horizontal (departmental) and vertical (institutional) levels (Brown, 1977).

---

[1] Allan Tucker mentions twenty-eight roles, including the roles of teacher, mentor, researcher, leader, and planner (Tucker, 1984, p. 4). The ninety-seven activities are reported in studies conducted at the University of Nebraska. Information about these studies is available from the authors.

Chairs assume their posts at a substantial cost to their professional interests and scholarly careers. Chairs have difficulty maintaining active lives as teachers or scholars. Moreover, they typically lack compensation for their chair duties, either in release time or dollars. A chair's length of appointment seldom extends beyond six years, causing institutions to under-utilize individuals with administrative talents and to create discontinuity in departmental leadership. Chair training in administration and leadership occurs primarily from on-the-job experience or from observing admired leaders. Like other academic administrators on campuses, departmental leaders

> do what we [they)]have either observed others do when they were in these roles or emulate, incorrectly, some other shadowy figures of the past, fantasies of Harvard Business School products, General Patton, creatures of fiction or movies, or some atavisms of leadership and authority which never were (Bennis, 1973, p. 397).

Chairpersons are appointed by administrators or elected by faculty for offices to which they may neither aspire nor seek. Kenneth Eble, a former English chairperson and perceptive observer of academic departments, has commented:

> Those who want the position are often ruled out for their wanting it. Those who don't want it are often, and unwisely forced into it. Those who assume the office must face a disdain for administration from many of their colleagues and even from themselves (1986, p. 2).

Their busy lives as chairs and their lack of training preclude investing substantial time in assisting faculty. Reflection upon your *own* career will help you recognize that other professionals played a significant role. Thus the journey toward helping others begins with an assessment of your *own* career.

The Nature of the Department

Over the years supporters and critics have argued the merits of academic departments on college campuses. Arguing the advantages of these units, Andersen cited five reasons for viewing the department as a legitimate unit:

> 1.   Departments provide the milieu most suitable for the development, preservation, and transmission of knowledge.
>
> 2.   Departments have the familiarity, formal simplicity, and clearly defined hierarchy of authority to which students and instructors can easily relate.

3. Departments serve faculty as a unit where they can interact with a minimum of misunderstanding and superfluous effort.

4. Departments serve as a protective unit for the faculty within the college or university organization.

5. Departments provide an understandable and workable status system within which the faculty member can be oriented and professionally evaluated (Andersen, 1977, pp. 8-9).

Despite these advantages for both chairs and faculty, the nature of academic departments creates difficulties for establishing a positive faculty work environment. Departments inhibit the development of new fields of knowledge, contribute to the isolation of professors, and promote unnecessary narrow specialization of courses and research (Andersen, 1977). These factors cause chairs to have difficulty in building faculty support for departmental goals and directions. Individuals become advocates for their own narrow specializations. Departments withdraw into themselves and become isolated. Departmental strength and vitality seem to be waxing and waning. Above all else, academic departments are not viewed by the personnel within them as logical units where faculty growth and development occur. It is easier and more convenient to displace this responsibility to faculty development centers, faculty committees, and academic deans. A need exists for chairs to consider how they can capitalize on the strengths of departments in promoting a positive work environment for faculty.

The Faculty Work Condition

Interaction between chairs and faculty is both a source of satisfaction and frustration. Faculty want autonomy but request assistance, demand quick decisions yet belabor issues, seek power and authority but delegate decisions to administrators. Years of academic freedom have bred a work force of rugged individualists, people who "vary widely in competencies, goals, energy, and general crankiness" (Eble, 1986, p. 2).

National reports about professors portray a discouraging picture of academic life on many college campuses today. We know that in recent years faculty work conditions have changed and even deteriorated on many campuses. A Carnegie Foundation for the Advancement of Teaching survey of five thousand faculty reported that 41 percent of the faculty were less enthusiastic about their work now than when they began their academic careers. When asked about morale in departments, 75 percent responded that it is worse today than five years ago (Boyer, 1987). A study of faculty and administrators in thirty-three institutions by Howard Bowen and Jack Schuster of Claremont Graduate School indicated an 11.7

percent decline in the real dollar earnings of the instructional staff from 1970-71 to 1983-84 (Bowen and Schuster, 1986). In terms of an aging faculty, they projected a need for new professors during the years 1985 to 2009 equal to two-thirds or more of the total number of faculty working in 1985 (Bowen and Schuster, 1986). These issues -- loss of enthusiasm, lowered morale, loss of real dollar earnings, an aging faculty -- are only a few of the issues facing the American professoriate today, but they provide more than sufficient reason to reflect on the working conditions of college faculty and to consider steps necessary to improve the situation.

A need exists for each chairperson to better understand the situation of faculty in his or her department with an eye toward intervening unobtrusively in ways that will facilitate good interpersonal communication with their staff and enable faculty to grow and develop.

A Self-Assessment

Before proceeding in this book, we suggest that readers complete the self-assessment checklist below. If you are a faculty member, consider whether the questions apply to your chairperson.

The list is not meant to exhaust all possible situations. It focuses on key issues or concerns identified by chairs in our study and directs the reader to specific passages in the book that might be helpful. After completing the assessment and reviewing strategies mentioned in the following chapters, try a few of them. Later, return to Chapter Ten of the book and review whether you have followed the four dimensions of the building process.

About the Self-Development of Chairs (See Chapter Two, pp. 9-20)

Answer each of the following with a yes or a no.

___1.   Do you feel that you have adequate knowledge about the department -- its history, strengths, mission, faculty, and students -- to be effective?

___2.   Have you built effective networks with other chairpersons and administrators on campus?

___3.   Do you engage in a balance of professional, personal, and leisure activities?

___4.   Do you have a plan for your career after serving as the chair?

___5.   Have you been able to keep current in your discipline or academic field?

About Leading an Academic Department (See Chapter Three, pp. 21-30)

___6.   Has your department developed a clear vision for the future of the department?

___7.   Do the faculty demonstrate ownership of and commitment to this vision?

___8.   Do you have an ongoing process to identify areas that are in need of change?

___9.   Is the process for the allocation of resources clearly understood by the faculty within the department?

___10.   Is the department data base adequate to provide the information you need to make decisions?

About Interacting Positively with Faculty (See Chapter Four, pp. 31-44)

___11.   Do faculty in the department perceive that there is an open, supportive atmosphere or climate?

___12.   Have you found your listening skills to be effective?

___13.   Do you regularly assist faculty in setting realistic goals and priorities?

___14.   Do you provide feedback to faculty about their performance in the areas of teaching, research, and scholarship?

___15.   Are faculty aware of your role as an advocate for them with upper administration?

___16.   Do you find your mentoring activities to be effective with faculty?

___17.   Do you provide encouragement or reinforcement to faculty?

About the Process of Addressing Specific Faculty Issues

___18.   Do you have new faculty in your department who need to be oriented and acclimated to the unit? (See Chapter Five, pp. 47-59)

___19.   Are you looking for ways to improve the teaching performance of faculty? (See Chapter Six, pp. 60-70)

___20.   Do you need to improve the scholarly performance of faculty in your department? (See Chapter Seven, pp. 71-82)

___21.   Do you have faculty in the department who lack vitality and enthusiasm? (See Chapter Eight, pp. 83-93)

___22.   Is the performance of a faculty member being affected by personal problems? (See Chapter Nine, pp. 94-103)

About an Overall Plan for Positive Work Environment for Faculty

___23.   Are the activities you use in building a positive work environment for faculty within the department effective? (See Chapter Ten, pp. 104-114)

CHAPTER TWO

First, Consider
Your Own Development

*Without some self-
development, chairs
cannot be energized to
work with faculty [a
chairman of a social
sciences department].*

A prerequisite for enhancing the growth of faculty is to be growing yourself. This means that you see yourself in a dynamic growth process -- you are changing, maturing, looking for new insights, and reflecting on patterns of thought and behavior. It also means that you see yourself as learning and gaining from interactions with faculty. They have much to offer. You also see yourself moving beyond yourself and into the perceptual world of others. As writers in the counseling and helping fields recommend, to facilitate the careers of others you need to "know yourself" (Brammer, 1979).

This chapter will provide an opportunity for you to explore your own professional life. We discuss three strategies for chair self-development based on the observations of excellent chairpersons. To help faculty relate professional goals to departmental and institutional goals and missions, learn about your role and responsibilities as a chair. To be fresh, alert, and rested to help another person, balance your personal and professional lives. To assist individual faculty members plan their careers, review your own long-range career plans.

Reflect on three questions as you read this chapter:

1. How do chairs learn about the departmental and institutional context in which they work?

2. How do chairs balance their personal and professional lives?

3. How do chairs plan for their own careers as administrators or faculty?

Learn about your role and responsibilities in the department and the institution.

In a book sponsored by the Sloan Foundation, the prize-winning physicist Freeman Dyson describes a "sum-over-histories" way of looking at electrons, an original idea that has become slowly absorbed into the structure of physics:

> The electron does whatever it likes. The electron goes all over space and time in all possible ways. It can even go backward in time whenever it chooses. If you start with an electron in this state at a certain time and you want to see whether it will be in some other state at another time, you just add together contributions from all the possible histories of the electron that take it from this state to the other. . . . The same trick works with minor changes not only for electrons but for everything else - atoms, baseballs, elephants, and so on (1979, p. 10).

Like the particle scientist, chairpersons need to examine "all the possible histories" of an academic department. This can be accomplished by:

1. Interning with the present chair.

2. Preparing in advance for the chair position.

3. Learning where responsibilities begin and end.

4. Visiting with experienced chairs.

5. Developing good working relationships with deans and senior administrators.

Learning about the department will be easier if a chair has been a faculty member prior to assuming the new position. The ideal is to be groomed for the position over an extended period of time. A chairperson in education at a comprehensive university described an "internship" arrangement for in-house aspirants to the chairpersonship:

> In our department faculty usually know three years ahead that they will assume the position. During these three years, they've been included in budgeting, accreditation, professional conferences for chairs, and aspects of decision making.

Especially important for a new chair or an individual coming to the department from the outside is the "advance preparation" needed to understand the department and its faculty. A chair in forestry commented:

> Take enough time to become truly familiar with the department, its faculty, programs, research thrusts, strengths and weaknesses. I know that may be a luxury and may require a great deal of

effort, but try to find time. Those first few months can be terribly stressful. Advance preparation can help.

This advance preparation is important. Few chairs are given an orientation when they assume their position. In a study of thirty-nine department chairs, Bragg (1981) reported that 82 percent had no orientation to the job when they assumed the post: they simply received policy manuals and were given instructions to call if they had any questions.

How does one prepare in advance? Visit the department frequently and learn as much as possible about it before accepting a position. Analyze and study minutes of past departmental meetings, official institutional policies, and budget documents for the last few years. Review publications by faculty and examine student evaluations of teaching. Peruse program reviews or accreditation reports of the department. Read long-range planning documents and mission statements. Visit with faculty members to explore their general needs, interests, and perception of issues and problems facing the department.

Learning about the department also involves understanding your responsibilities and knowing when matters should be delegated to others. Chairpersons are called upon to solve many types of problems. James March, a nationally known authority on organizations, said that what distinguishes a good bureaucracy from a bad one is "how well it accomplishes the trivia of day-to-day relations with clients and day-to-day problems in maintaining and operating its technology" (1980, p. 17). Though department chairs may not characterize their units as bureaucracies, they would readily admit that they spend much time on minor day-to-day issues and problems. Before spending an inordinate amount of time on an issue, chairs might ask themselves: "Is this a problem I need to undertake, or should it be delegated to someone else?" As one individual commented, "You have to learn how to delegate authority, and you also have to learn what you are responsible for." In larger units, responsibilities can be delegated to vice-chairs or assistant chairpersons. In smaller units, the range of issues can be extensive, as a biological sciences chair in a small liberal arts college commented:

> If the bathrooms are not clean, who else is there to tell but the chair? If there are problems in the department, the chairperson has to accept the fact that she or he will become the sounding board for the problems. If the faculty are unhappy about something, the inclination is to tell the chair. You have to handle that and not be put off by it.

Learning about the department and the responsibility of chairing can be enhanced by visiting with experienced chairs who have solid reputations for success on campus and expertise in specific aspects of chairing. The following observations came from individuals new to the chair post as well as more experienced individuals:

> I recommend that people new to the position visit with other chairs. Seek out individuals who have been in the position and who have learned how things work in the institution. As you become more savvy about the political process, the budget, and the management processes involved in the institution, you become more effective [a new chair in the field of psychology with two years of experience].

> I really would have drowned here the first month if I didn't share a secretary with an individual who had been here for twenty years and who, in my mind, had been a superb chair for many of those years. The advice helped me to get my feet on the ground and to develop perspective [a new chair in social sciences with three years of experience].

The chairpersons suggested seeking out individuals with a reputation for expertise in specific aspects of chairing.

> Accept for one moment that you are not an administrative whiz kid, even if you think you are. Find the outstanding chairs at your institution and learn how they conduct evaluations. I can't emphasize enough how damaging a misspoken adjective can be on an evaluation or how productive a good evaluation can be [a chair in medical sciences with eight years of experience].

In addition to informal visits with experienced individuals, you may find a formal workshop on or off campus helpful. One chairperson described a regular event on his campus:

> The chairs of the departments meet to discuss important issues every month or six weeks. Some of the issues revolve around administrative responsibilities of the chairs. Recognizing variation in responsibilities and in functions due to the nature, history, and discipline of the units, we discuss a wide range of approaches.

Aside from other chairs, senior administrators such as deans and campus-wide officials can be helpful, too. A mathematics chair from a regional university somewhat facetiously said: "Make sure you have a good dean to work with." Unfortunately, the selection of the dean is normally out of the chair's hands. Nonetheless, explore the nature of administrative support for your unit and the management styles of other administrators. Learn these through formal experiences at work and through social, informal means.

It is crucial that senior administrators are committed to your department. "Make sure the university hierarchy is committed to your program and goals and convince them through performance and creative programs that you have the single most dynamic program on campus," said a major research university chair in communications. Study the management styles of senior administrators. Learn the strengths and weaknesses of people who make decisions affecting the department,

> The squeaky wheel gets the grease. The chair needs to learn how to "squeak" in a diplomatic way. There will be a pay-off if the approach is appropriate [a health, physical education and recreation chair in a regional doctoral-granting school].

> It's important for a chair to get to know the people who have some control over resources and who actually make decisions. Get to know the central administrators -- the vice presidents and the president -- where they're coming from, what they think, and what their motives are. This knowledge means more than becoming "acquainted" with them [a philosophy chair in a state college].

How does an individual become more than "acquainted" with senior administrators? Interact with them on projects and campus-based activities. An anthropology chair in a state college recommended attending social gatherings:

> I would definitely recommend that the chair go to parties and receptions. Enhance visibility; meet people outside of your discipline with whom you interact. It is tremendously important to see, for instance, that there are two sides to the vice president of the budget: one is when you are dealing with formal budget requests, the other is when you see the person at a social gathering.

Through these approaches, you enhance opportunities for departmental support. As one individual said: "If they throw money at you, you know things are okay."

Create a balance between your professional and personal life.

Someone has said it is impossible to be happy in only one aspect of life. Individuals in our study advised balancing personal time -- time with family, friends, and significant others -- with departmental time. A medical chairperson in a major research university talked about setting aside time for the family:

Look out for yourself. I'm amazed how many people assume chair responsibilities and then their personal lives fall apart with divorce or other problems. Chairs must take time to look out for their family relationships. They just can't drop it all. They shouldn't let the job overwhelm and inundate their personal time. They've got to say, "Okay, enough's enough. I'm spending the weekend with my family, and I'm not going to let anything interfere -- barring a major emergency."

Note the escape clause in the final phrase. Chairs could classify all departmental issues as major emergencies: "That faculty member's request can't wait until Monday!" "I must get the memos out!" "The budget must be completed over the weekend or we'll not receive the grant!" "Excellent" chairpersons recommended restraint in classifying issues as major emergencies.

The importance of a family commitment and the strength that can be derived from such an orientation was emphasized by two chairs. A relatively new chair in a small liberal arts institution said:

I think it works well to set aside specific time for personal needs. Families don't automatically have to suffer when an individual assumes the chair. I know a lot of colleagues whose good marriages fell apart when they became chair. I'm sure chairs are well above the national average in the divorce rate. I have four children. Although I wouldn't give myself accolades, I think I have held my family commitment together pretty well.

"It is easy to get caught in the trap of overemphasizing the importance of the department," said a five-year veteran chair in a social sciences department.

Some chairs let their families go. They get enough ego boost from their job that they let their families fall apart. Still, they keep on working and it doesn't bother them. But it can be devastating in the long run. I think my family actually allows me to do a better job. I'm fresher, more alert, and have a better attitude if I'm not inundated with my department for ninety-nine hours a week, fifty-two weeks of the year.

Personal time can be increased by using common sense methods for being more efficient at the job. Chairs handle considerable paper work and small chores sometimes called "administrivia." Reports must be prepared, memos written, inquiries answered, telephone calls returned, students registered, budgets developed, and class schedules organized.

You can profit from time-saving techniques. "Get petty, necessary things done quickly so you can concentrate on the important things," commented one chairperson. Others had more specific solutions: "Get an answering machine to help reduce the amount of time consumed or utilized on the telephone," or "Develop the ability to deal with a lot of little things all at once," or "Become a 'list maker,' an 'organizer,' a 'facilitator.' Grease the wheel so things will work that aren't necessarily working." Chairs recommended similar approaches for handling paperwork:

> Don't get bogged down in paperwork. Make sure you can see the big picture -- where the department is going and what the faculty needs. If you can't figure out how to get paperwork off your desk, delegate someone else to handle it [a chairperson in plant sciences].

> I don't like paperwork. I try to do it as quickly as possible so I have it around for a minimal period of time [a chairperson in chemical engineering].

> Concentrate on making sure the paper flows [a chairperson in the social sciences].

Effective chairs are organized individuals who keep the paperwork flowing, use time-saving methods in their jobs, and have time for their personal life.

Another aspect of balance is to set aside time for activities that provide personal time. Physical exercise, for example, can provide a "mental break" in routine and contribute to a fresh and alert mind.

> Try to keep yourself physically fit. I think you have to set aside certain times for exercise. Go bicycling at 9:00 AM or to the university recreation facilities and work out from 3:00 to 4:00 P. M. Ask your secretary to map time out on your calendar, especially when you have heavily scheduled weeks and when you know you need a mental break [a chairperson in a liberal arts college].

Oftentimes, inexperienced chairs fear that they will be chastised by faculty for their exercise breaks. One chair disagreed with this assessment:

> I've never gotten flack from the faculty and the department for taking time off for physical activity. If anything, faculty respect me for keeping myself in good physical condition. I think I'm more physically and mentally alert because of it. I'm not talking about people who put thirty hours a week into fitness. I'm talking about an honest three hours a week, half of which conflicts with the time I'm expected to be in the office. Too many young chairs get started and then just fall apart with high blood pressure or family problems.

This individual not only gained faculty "respect" for time away from the office, he also benefited from being more alert because of his physical regimen.

Prepare for your professional future.

"Do I plan to return to a primary professional career as a teacher or researcher or become involved in administrative activities on a permanent basis?" "What activities give me the greatest satisfaction - leadership and management, or scholarly activities such as teaching, research, and service?" "What will I do once I have completed my tenure as chairperson?"

These questions remind us of the fourteenth lesson advanced by Gregory Kimble in his *Department Chairpersons' Survival Manual* (1979, p. 4). "Prepare for your own demise as chairman." Assessing and planning for the future represents an integral part of a chair's self-development.

An earth sciences chairperson in a doctoral-granting school used the term "soul search" to describe this assessment:

> If you want to assume a chairmanship, do a soul search. Determine whether your career plans are to remain a faculty member or a researcher or to move up administratively. In some of the hard sciences like biology, for example, a chairmanship can very often ruin a research career. However, if the person wants to move up administratively, the chair position would be a good step.

Though the chair post may place your teaching and research activities "on hold," it also opens opportunities for an administrative career. Regardless whether you pursue administration or decide to later return to the faculty, assessing your long-range professional goals helps maintain appropriate professional priorities during your term in office.

Unless this "soul search" is done, holding the position can jeopardize an academic career.

The chair position should not be a dead end. I've known several chairs who didn't have anywhere to go after their terms. They didn't move up in administration; maybe they didn't want to. But they hadn't sufficiently planned ahead for their own careers [chairman of a social science department in a research university].

Chairpersons who eventually plan to return to full-time teaching or research after their service as chair can enhance a successful return by maintaining an intellectual focus in their discipline or field of study or by "retooling" before assuming another faculty post. An individual in social sciences at a research university said, "Maintain your stature as a scholar. Be concerned with your own professional activities." Although this may be especially true for people in research institutions, a chairperson in a liberal arts college made a similar comment:

I would advise chairs that keeping themselves intellectually alive is the most important thing for their overall growth and development. Chairs must be involved in some challenging intellectual focus in both teaching and in their field.

A chair in a social sciences department in a research university metaphorically described the heavy "service" demands of chairing:

A chair has to pay a lot of attention to how she develops as a scholar. Pay attention to the edge and notice if the edge is getting dull. The chair is a service job in many ways. That service is immensely affected by whether the chair is developing or achieving as a scholar.

Professional activities or "retooling" as a scholar may be less important for an individual who aspires to a higher administrative position after serving as chair. If a person's career direction is unknown, it is best to keep both options open -- to remain active professionally in scholarly activities and to learn as much as possible about academic leadership.

Extensive time demands make it difficult to maintain an edge as a scholar or teacher. Whether the career path will be administration, teaching, or research, consider "saving time for yourself and maintaining some degree of equilibrium in your own work." This calls for an agenda. Careful attention to scheduling classes and meetings can create blocks of time for concentrated scholarly activities and for teaching. Scheduling time for scholarly work was emphasized by one chairperson with eight years of experience in the hard sciences from a doctoral-granting school:

> Chairs must learn to organize their time. One can always find things to do -- shuffle papers, make another report. It's very important that a chair have a project always hanging overhead that will keep him in touch with his profession -- it could be a research project or something administrative, but something where continuous ideas are needed.

Without a definite agenda, administrative tasks can consume much time. Creating "equilibrium" between one's career discipline and the duties of chairing a department becomes difficult because the demands of leadership always exceed the time available. Thus, "excellent" chairpersons advised planning for the future by choosing a career path, maintaining an intellectual focus for work or "retooling," and scheduling time for professional, discipline-based activities.

Suggested Resources

Books

Bennett, J.B. *Managing the Academic Department.* New York: American
      Council on Education - Macmillan Publishing Company, 1983.

John Bennett's book contains case studies of specific faculty and department situations. Intended to help department heads or chairs learn constructive reactions to departmental problems. Chapters containing case studies include discussion of responsibilities, conflict, performance counseling, departmental change, decisions, and other special situations. "Performance Counseling" case studies are concerned with teaching, course assignment and curriculum, working with teaching assistants, and faculty career problems.

Booth, D.B. *The Department Chair: Professional Development and
      Role Conflict.* AAHE-ERIC Higher Education Research Report
      10, 1982. Washington D.C.: American Association for Higher
      Education, 1982.

David Booth's fifty-three-page book includes discussion of administrative aspects of chairing a department. "The Chair at Work" section includes commentary on role conflict, ambiguity, and how the chair learns the job.

Kimble, G.A. *A Departmental Chairperson's Survival Manual.* New
York: John Wiley & Sons, 1979.

Gregory Kimble has prepared this book for chairpersons in psychology
departments. This manual resulted from workshops conducted by the Council of
Graduate Departments of Psychology. Content is pertinent to all disciplines.
Readers will be amused, elated, or saddened by Kimble's observations. Don't
miss the introductory "Letter to a New Chairman." It contains fourteen lessons
starting with the idea: "As head of a department, you must be prepared to budget
between one-fourth and one-half of your time for the totally unexpected" (p. 4).

Tucker, A. *Chairing the Academic Department: Leadership Among
Peers.* New York: American Council on Education -Macmillan
Publishing Company, 1984.

Allan Tucker offers an extensive discussion of the role of chairing an
academic department. *Chairing an Academic Department*, now in its second
edition, has benefited from Dr. Tucker's extensive experience in workshops for
department chairpersons sponsored by the American Council on Education. The
book covers the spectrum of departmental responsibilities and has become a
classic in this field. We recommend special attention to the chapters on faculty
development, evaluation, performance counseling, and grievances.

Newsletters

Academic Leader (published monthly by Magna Publications).

The *Academic Leader* provides practical tips about chairing departments
and brief discussions of research studies. Inquiries may be directed to Magna
Publications, Inc., 607 N. Sherman Ave., Madison, WI 53704.

The Department Advisor (published four times a year by Higher
Education Executive Publications, Inc. in affiliation with the
American Council on Education, Center for Leadership
Development.)

This newsletter includes original articles "providing concrete analyses
and practical advice to help department chairs do their jobs." Contact *The
Department Advisor*, P.O. Box 12635, Denver, Colorado 80212.

Eble, K. E. "Chairpersons and Faculty Development" in John Bennett, Ed. *The Department Advisor* Denver, CO: Higher Education Executive Publications, 1986.

Kenneth Eble was one of two contributors to this issue of *The Department Advisor*. Eble reports and reflects upon his examination of chairpersons and their interests in faculty development at forty-one colleges in Minnesota, North Dakota, and South Dakota. Traditional faculty development practices are discussed. Eble suggests chairperson involvement in faculty development, an involvement extending beyond traditional sabbaticals, travel funds, and grant writing support. After discussing the reasons people become chairpersons and the skills necessary for the position, the author suggests ways that chairpersons should work with faculty members, e.g., let faculty members know that their work is important, let them know that they are contributing to the department and the institution.

National Workshops

There are Academic Chairperson Conferences held annually by Kansas State University's Center for Faculty Evaluation and Development. (Contact the Center for Faculty Evaluation and Development, Division of Continuing Education, 1623 Anderson Avenue, Manhattan, Kansas 66502-4098.) Additionally, the American Association for Higher Education's Annual Conference (Contact AAHE, One Dupont Circle, Suite 600, Washington D.C. 20036.) and the American Council on Education's Department Leadership Program (ACE, One Dupont Circle, Eighth Floor, Washington D.C. 20036-1193) provide occasional workshops for departmental chairs.

CHAPTER THREE

Reflect on Your Role as an Academic Leader

We assume that you are an academic leader in the department -- an individual primarily responsible for creating the work environment. What strategies can you use to assist the entire department to grow and develop so that faculty members' careers are enhanced?

Given the diverse interests and specializations of faculty in departments, you present and discuss a unifying focus for the department that responds to faculty needs. You recognize that faculty seek to be independent and you consider approaches for building faculty ownership of ideas. Part of the independent streak in faculty is their need to be brought along slowly and deliberately. You are sensitive to their needs in this process. You recognize that they view you as one who can obtain resources and present their best side through reports and information disseminated outside the department. This chapter will present strategies based on terms such as vision, ownership, change, resources, and monitoring progress.

Reflect on five questions as you read this chapter:

1. How do chairs establish a collective vision or focus with faculty for the department;

2. How do chairs develop faculty ownership of the vision;

3. How do chairs initiate change, assuming that changes need to be made in the department;

4. How do chairs use resources available to facilitate implementing the vision; and

5. How do chairs monitor progress of the department and faculty toward accomplishing the vision.

Establish a collective departmental vision or focus.

Two national authorities on leadership, Warren Bennis and Burt Nanus (1985, p. 89) describe vision as a "mental image of a possible and desirable future state of the organization .... [It] may be as vague as a dream or as precise as a goal or mission statement." Chairpersons in our study described vision as "an active focus on the future rather than the past"; "keeping in mind one axiom -- what will be the best for the department, the students, and the curriculum over the long haul"; and "setting sights on long-term goals, recognizing that a chair can get pushed in so many different directions."

You need to relate the departmental vision to the mission of the institution. What is the current focus of the college or university? Historically, what have been the major thrusts of the college or university? What has the college or university identified for future directions? What types of programs will be supported internally and externally? Answering these questions requires a clear vision of the mission of the unit and the entire institution. Without this, chairs said, "false expectations and unrealistic goals can be established for the faculty and for the department which can result in conflict and lack of support from upper administration." Instead, chairs must, "help [the faculty] understand and appreciate the mission of the institution."

Although the faculty member needs freedom to pursue individual career interests, those individual pursuits must be linked and related in a meaningful way to the broader institutional mission. Like the conductor of a symphony, chairs orchestrate the resolution of needs and the setting of priorities for the enhancement of individual and institutional goals. This dynamic was described by an education chairperson in a comprehensive college:

> Faculty must have freedom to determine where their efforts will be expended. There are many things a faculty member can do that satisfy the individual as well as benefit the institution. The job of the administrator is to help determine ways faculty can help themselves and simultaneously help the institution. The chair is in a key position to make this happen.

Faculty members experience satisfaction when their efforts are appreciated at the institutional level and when senior administrators can view the faculty member's contribution as significant to the institution rather than self-serving.

Develop faculty ownership of the vision.

A vision cannot be unilaterally determined by the chair, because the academy is built on a foundation of participation and involvement of faculty in matters related to governance, staffing, students, budgeting, and academic programs. Bennis and Nanus state the case:

> A vision cannot be established in an organization by edict or by the exercise of power or coercion. It is more an act of persuasion, of creating an enthusiastic and dedicated commitment

to a vision because it is right for the times, right for the organization, and right for the people who are working in it (p. 107).

Struggle a bit with your own thoughts and reactions to the following questions before reading the strategies of "excellent" chairs.

*What changes are necessary within the department?

*What mechanisms and structures exist for generating ideas?

*How can I get the faculty interested in considering and owning ideas?

The chairs in our study mentioned several strategies that worked well for them. A biomedical engineering chairperson visited with faculty before meetings and allowed everyone to state his or her views on issues. "I drop into offices chatting, huddle fashion," he said. "This way faculty come to meetings primed for the issue." The chair's visit with faculty in this department builds consensus among the faculty members, contributing to ownership. As faculty in the department commented:

> We have a good consensus on issues but he still allows the department to outvote him. Before we meet, issues are brought up. We try not to let decisions be made on a close vote. He (the chair) goes around and talks before the meeting. We're generally aware of opportunities, and he makes assignments based on interests and strengths.

> When we have a faculty meeting he doesn't say, "I am the head and this is what we will do." He sets the spirit and runs these meetings through consensus. Clockwise around the table, everyone comments, and then we reach a consensus. If consensus doesn't emerge, the decision is put off until more time can be spent considering it.

Building ownership through a consensus model at meetings was only one approach recommended. An education chairperson at a liberal arts institution emphasized the importance of a *nondirective* approach:

> Anyone who comes with an agenda, a leadership vision of what faculty ought to be, will have a hard time. There will be resistance to that management style. You need to listen to

faculty; they are professionals. They know their own areas best. The chair, in my opinion, needs to represent and be responsive to faculty rather than being directive.

Another individual emphasized the role of a *catalyst*:

You can't do it by yourself. You need faculty support for developing a vision. Some faculty committee or group of committees must be given responsibility to assist with development. There's no way I could run all the programs in this department. The ownership of ideas has to be in the hands of faculty.

The ownership of ideas through *faculty initiation* is reinforced by a chairperson in a research institution who said: "Don't do anything your faculty did not initiate. Remember the bubble-up theory -- nothing should be done that doesn't come from the faculty." Faculty feel ownership when they see some *benefits* for themselves. A chairperson in a large department commented:

The department has to be a unit with everyone working together, moving forward together, benefiting together, although in different ways depending on individual needs and interests. Some faculty might not see benefits immediately or how the program contributes to their development at a given point in time, but eventually they must be able to see the implications.

One person emphasized the importance of *identity* and *social contacts* in building ownership in a large department of ninety faculty at a research institution:

We've tried to do things to keep a sense of cohesive community working together in a department of this size. We've posted everybody's picture along with their area of responsibility in a prominent place in the department. This might sound trivial, but people have been pleased. In addition, we started having informal social hours every few weeks. People just drop in and talk to one another. These practices actually seem to enhance people's sense of belonging to a group rather than just coming in and doing their thing and then going home.

A chairman of a theater department at a major university *shared* his vision on a regular basis with his faculty.

The chair of a department of theater is also the artistic director of the theater program. Thus, I believe in not only having a

vision for the program but also sharing that vision. One way I
share this vision is to write to my faculty on a regular basis my
thoughts about our departmental vision. I have -- at least every
semester -- a meeting in which we talk simply about vision. As
we have become increasingly trusting and ready to engage in
discussion, I've discovered that my desire to share has been
quite infectious.

These comments make it clear that the chairperson who is successful in developing
faculty ownership will elicit support and commitment.

Initiate changes slowly.

Be cautious about making immediate changes. Allow considerable time
to let ideas mature and develop naturally. Most department procedures have a
long history, but changes are sometimes needed if the vision or direction of the
department needs to be altered. Chairs advised "no quick fixes." This sage
advice contradicts the popular "100-day theory" in management circles, that is,
to make changes during the 100-day "honeymoon" period.

The following quotes provide specific suggestions about change --
getting acquainted, listening, moving slowly, and making one change at a time:

Hang loose. Spend time observing and getting acquainted. Do
not do too much in the first year. Set plans. Don't apply
formulas until you know what you're dealing with. Praise
people; listen to them. Get acquainted with the faculty and the
department before you decide what needs to be done [a social
sciences chairperson with ten years of experience].

Don't change too much too soon. If you don't have an
administrative background, it takes at least a year to become
familiar with your responsibilities. Visit with other chairs to see
how they handle various situations. Try to read as much as
possible about management [an accounting chairperson with
sixteen years of experience].

You can't change the world overnight. It takes six months just
to figure out what is important to the faculty and the department
[a psychology chairperson with eight years of experience].

> Try not to build Rome in a day. The task of changing the department is too big to be accomplished in a short period of time. Look at departmental change as a long-term commitment. Take progress as it comes, capitalizing on the opportunities which emerge [a chairperson in medicine with eight years of experience].

The advice was consistent:

1. Let things evolve naturally and slowly.

2. Spend time the first year observing and getting acquainted.

3. Visit with other chairs to see how they handle situations.

4. Look at the new "vision" as a long-term commitment.

Being slow and deliberate, however, doesn't mean abnegating responsibility. Chairpersons were firm in their counsel to take action immediately when merited by a situation.

Allocate resources of time, information, and assignments to encourage the vision.

Whether implementing changes or continuing along a steady course, departmental leaders can exercise the power and influence of their position to encourage a vision. While this power depends on many factors -- foremost the degree of administrative latitude over the budget -- most chairs exercise at least modest control over departmental resources such as funds, information, and faculty assignments. As one chair commented, "The most basic thing that any faculty member needs is the resources to do her work. That's my biggest responsibility."

If a department has control over its budget, you can allocate funds that provide immeasurable aid to faculty, such as moneys for secretarial assistance, costs for computer time, funds for travel, and resources for equipment purchases. Though the "excellent" chairs talked about these traditional uses of funds, they also spoke about incentives, rewards, and equitable treatment of faculty. One chair did not mince words: "Reward things that you want done." Others talked about allocating funds at the right place and time as incentives for faculty.

> Good management requires having resources in the right place at the right time [a chairperson in an anthropology department with twenty-two faculty].

Try to find resources that will enable people to do what they need to do [a chairperson in genetics with eight faculty].

Give faculty resources so that they can maximize their effort [a chairperson in marketing with fourteen faculty].

Faculty can be rewarded by fair and equitable distribution of salary. This may involve negotiating faculty needs with upper administration. A chair in languages and literature in a doctoral-granting institution explained:

You have to determine quickly the salary structure in the department. Determine how you can reward those faculty members who in previous administrations were not given the increments deserved -- for whatever reasons. Then you have to convince the faculty and the dean it's a good idea to allow equity to prevail. Again, you will receive respect of the faculty -- something that you need if you're going to be successful.

Chairpersons in our study were great "information givers," passing along information to faculty -- another resource within your power and influence. The chair's office is a clearinghouse for materials of substantial interest to faculty: notices about meetings, announcements of available grants and contracts, and information about campus committees, events, and resources. The following quotes demonstrate the range of possibilities:

Once you have a feeling for what faculty prefer to do, you can start guiding materials towards them.

Keep abreast of the periodicals and what is new. Pass this information along to the faculty.

I try to put something in every faculty member's mailbox every day.

Try to get as many sources of information as possible to your faculty.

Help new faculty become aware of sources of support such as institutional resources and faculty aid programs.

Another resource for faculty is time -- time to work on a favorite project, to take a "breather" from the routine of teaching or research, to refocus efforts. Part of the difficulty in allocating this resource is convincing upper administration of the need. A chairperson in a doctoral-granting institution stressed this point:

> I think you have to work very hard to convince the administration that faculty need released time in order to publish, research, and provide service. You also have to find ways to be flexible in providing time to the faculty member.

Numerous practices emerged from our interviews about managing time to the advantage of faculty. Sabbatical leaves and released time for additional graduate training, professional preparation, and research were the most often cited practices, but chairs also said:

> I assigned first-year faculty members to teach in comfortable areas to lessen their load.

> We try to trade courses and research to get more teaching in a particular year and less teaching later.

> We try to avoid having too many faculty meetings. We only meet three times a year.

> I try to get out of the way of faculty and let them do their jobs.

> We believe in taking administrative tasks from faculty so they can do their faculty jobs.

> I give individuals time off to attend workshops.

As this partial list suggests, you can complement traditional faculty development activities by allocating time such development requires.

Monitor progress toward achieving the vision.

"Academic leaders" also monitor individual and departmental progress toward goals or a vision. Chairs should consider organizing procedures and data systems which indicate performance levels of faculty and staff. Ownership and involvement of faculty in establishing and developing these systems often falls to the chairperson.

An effective data base should be simple yet comprehensive, covering the major activities in a department. Data bases can become so complex and costly to maintain that they result in information overload. A chairperson of a biosciences department in a comprehensive institution offered several tips:

> Get the departmental data bases in order -- for students, courses,
> published works, grants, and awards. Get on top of the problems
> with the curriculum. Sort out the new and the emerging
> curriculum. Have a means to assess and determine those
> courses which need to be dropped.

Consider building a data base of basic information about faculty performance. A chairperson in special education discussed collecting faculty data:

> Be adroit at picking information systems. Collect data on
> performance of the faculty, the effectiveness of the instruction
> provided by the department, the impact of resources provided,
> and the credit hour production. Try to be trusting while at the
> same time collecting data to document evidence of performance.

Faculty information has a myriad of uses, including pinpointing trends, tracing departmental history, and drawing comparisons both within the institution and with similar departments at other institutions. Instructional cost analysis reports -- departmental and institutional -- can assist chairpersons making decisions about faculty assignments, the allocation of resources and credit hours produced.

Once the data bases are developed, proper maintenance will ensure timely information for many purposes. Updating a data base in the midst of a crisis is often too late. The systems are important not only in providing information and documenting performance but also in identifying potential problems. A biology chairperson in a research university spoke of this concern:

> Know what is going on in the department so that you may head
> off potential problems before they emerge. You will be able to
> make better decisions.

One of the most satisfying experiences for a chair is to have access to both summative and formative evidence documenting progress of work toward specified objectives and goals.

Suggested Resources

Books

Bennis, W. and Nanus, B. *Leaders: The Strategies for Taking Charge.*
  New York: Harper & Row, Publishers, 1985.

We recommend this short paperback book for readers interested in the concept of vision and setting futuristic goals for an organization. Warren Bennis and Burt Nanus discuss developing and implementing visions that relate to departmental or unit concerns without ignoring the larger organizational context. Implementing a vision requires the modeling of behavior and providing active support for the vision. The authors suggest establishing a vision or agenda that will focus the attention of employees in an organization. One part of their discussion, "The Leader's Search for Commitment" (p. 106), reinforces the importance of a vision being "claimed" by those involved, a concept similar to ownership.

Heider, J. *The Tao of Leadership: Leadership Strategies for a New Age.*
  New York: Bantam Books, 1985.

The slow, natural enactment of change in a department, is exemplified in a short, entertaining book about leadership by J. Heider drawn from the writings of Lao Tzu, the fifth-century B.C. Chinese author of the *Tao Te Ching. Tao Te Ching* is a book of wise sayings, many of which will be familiar to you, e.g., "The journey of a thousand miles begins with a single step." Heider includes eighty-one lessons, such as "Selflessness," "Unbiased Leadership," "Take It Easy," "Gentle Interventions," and the "Unfolding Process."

Kouzes, J.M., and Posner, B.Z. *The Leadership Challenge: How to Get*
  Extraordinary Things Done in Organizations. San Francisco:
  Jossey-Bass, 1988.

James Kouzes and Barry Posner provide an excellent and insightful addition to the extensive array of management and leadership literature. Part Three, especially "Inspiring a Shared Vision," is recommended. The authors emphasized steps involved in visualizing an ideal future and in sharing the vision with members of your organization. The book contains seven parts -- understanding the roles of leaders and followers, initiating change in an organization, creating a vision, modeling desired behavior, encouraging productivity, and developing leaders.

CHAPTER FOUR

Create a Positive Interpersonal Work Environment

One doesn't have the option of choosing to ignore or pull away from faculty. Choices are more limited. The question is how to interact [a chairperson in education at a research university].

> *Find out what's going on out there and play to it. Support it. Nurture it. Utilize techniques which are appropriate to the personalities and the characteristics of the faculty you're working with. There is no universal formula. You have to individualize [a chairperson in a department of philosophy at a research institution].*

Understanding one's self and serving faculty as an academic leader are two essential components for a chair who supports and encourages faculty in their professional careers. Equally important is the challenge of positive interpersonal communications with faculty. Consider how you will relate to faculty needs in group settings like department meetings. Consider how you will assess their professional needs in one-on-one interactions such as goals and objectives sessions at the beginning of the year or performance reviews at the end of the year. In both group or individual settings, you can facilitate a good interpersonal environment.

Reflect on seven questions as you read this chapter:

1. How do chairs establish an "open" atmosphere that will build trust with the faculty?

2. What steps are involved in listening to faculty needs, interests, and aspirations?

3. How do chairs assist faculty in setting professional goals?

4. How do chairs provide positive feedback to enhance the pride and self-esteem of the faculty member?

5. How do chairpersons advocate and represent faculty to colleagues and senior administrators?

6. How do chairs model for or mentor faculty?

7. How do chairs encourage and support faculty?

Establish an open atmosphere to build trust.

It is important to create and maintain a collaborative, open, fair atmosphere, one in which there is a sense of caring about the development of the faculty as a primary function of the job. The chair has a lot to do with the atmosphere that is established [a chair from a liberal arts college].

Though faculty members vary considerably in needs and in abilities to contribute to a supportive environment, chairpersons can promote a positive, open departmental attitude. One chair called it "atmospheric guidance." This point was aptly stressed by a chairperson in chemical engineering at a doctoral-granting institution: "Set the proper framework and appropriate work environment so that faculty have a positive attitude toward their jobs."

What constitutes this "framework?" Excellent chairs talked about openness, trust, and honesty. Openness means creating a situation where faculty are free to express their views without threat of retaliation or reprisal. The chairs cited several ways to achieve or maintain openness, including respecting minority views, seeking everyone's input, keeping faculty informed about what was going on, avoiding the perception of competing with faculty, and being forthright in discussing institutional expectations with faculty. The chair in a department of civil engineering at a research university used the metaphor of a "family" to describe a workplace where faculty freely shared their ideas:

Consider the environment of the department as a family. All are equally important to the whole system. Ask their help to be a part of the enterprise and help fine-tune it. Everyone's input should be respected.

Besides respecting input, the chairs expressed the importance of participation and involvement: "Everyone should feel that they know what is going on and that they have a voice in it."

It is difficult to be open on all matters. The chair of a department of social sciences in a liberal arts college described his frustrations:

The chair has a continuing responsibility to maintain openness with the faculty. However, it is extremely difficult because you constantly find yourself being pressured to make quick decisions on items which need faculty discussion.

By limiting discussion, faculty may perceive the chair as operating in a closed, mistrusting manner. Sometimes the chair is caught on the horns of a major dilemma: to promote discussion on the one hand and to make a decision prior to having faculty input on the other. The safest course is to solicit faculty views before a decision is made. If this is impossible, then apologize or at least provide faculty with an explanation after the fact.

Encouraging openness helps establish trust with the faculty. Carl Rogers, a popular psychologist, pointed out the symbiotic relationship between openness and trust: trusting someone leads to a willingness to be open with that person; likewise, feeling trusted leads to openness (Rogers, 1961). A psychologist-chair in our project described his view of the relationship between openness and "trust":

> I run the most open department that I can think of. The only thing that I won't talk about are personal matters that would damage someone. I tell my faculty, "If I don't tell you what you want to know, ask me." If you don't have the faculty's trust, you're in trouble.

A chair in accounting in a comprehensive college mentioned the importance of people working together to build trust:

> Keep all people working together for organizational goals and objectives. Develop trust at all levels and avoid adversarial relations with superiors and subordinates.

While maintaining openness may sound easy, it is in fact quite difficult, especially in large departments. For example, faculty are normally interested in the budget process and how allocations are made in the department. In such a situation, what the chairperson tells the faculty about the budget determines to a large extent how faculty view the department in terms of openness. If faculty do not understand and appreciate how the funds are being expended, suspicion and distrust may follow.

Faculty expect to and should be informed, not surprised by the implementation of significant changes. Two psychology chairs referred to this as being "honest".

> Be honest and straightforward with your faculty. I tell my faculty that if they ever come up for promotion, tenure, or reappointment and they're surprised [with my expectations], I haven't done my job. They should never be surprised because I should be absolutely honest with them about the expectations and the requirements.

An open, trusting, and honest atmosphere promotes a positive work environment and a spirit of collegiality. Chairs can build this spirit through genuine attempts to share decision making. Numerous suggestions were given on how to avoid being perceived as a heavy-handed authority figure in the department:

> Be a colleague, not a dictator. Work as a team.

> Faculty can't work well in a dictatorial situation. Be an arbitrator and mediator.

> Be a facilitator, not a foreman. Establish a willingness to be giving and generous whenever possible.

> I must emphasize quite strongly that you can't whip faculty into line. You're not a factory foreman.

> I think people resent a chairperson, particularly a young one, if they come in and try to be a first lieutenant or captain or something like that.

> Don't be pushy. Get to know faculty as people. Pay attention to needs. Take them out to lunch. Let them know they're important as individuals.

Respecting individual views, keeping faculty informed about expectations and what is going on, and letting them share in making decisions are all practices that promote an open atmosphere in the department and build trusting relationships with faculty.

Listen to faculty needs and interests.

All people probably need to work on their listening skills. Faculty members may be reluctant to talk freely with the chairperson because of experiences with past leaders whom they felt did not listen or were unwilling to accept different points of view. If this situation exists, extra effort will be required. A basic principal of "excellent" chairpersons was to "reach out to *each* faculty member, not just to the complainers or to those supporting your views."

> I would listen, listen, listen. My strongest piece of advice is to keep your door open and reach out to each faculty member --

even the ones whom you think are doing well [a political science chairperson in a doctoral-granting school].

The following brief scenario cross-references "excellent" chair ideas with those of a leading authority on listening skills, Madelyn Burley-Allen (1982, pp. 96-98). Burley-Allen recommends that you work at listening by practicing with a number of people in your work unit.

Assume that you are a chairperson in a small department of ten faculty. A faculty member wants to talk to you about her "teaching problems." Her student evaluations were low in one course last semester. What steps would you take to listen to her? The following steps are suggested:

1. *Put the individual talking to you at ease.* As soon as you come into the faculty member's office, "Make faculty feel comfortable talking to you. Listen to what they have to say and be frank in your responses to their inquiry" (an architectural chair in a research university). One technique recommended by Burley-Allen is to start the conversation by discussing an area of common interest. Since both you and the faculty member are engaged in teaching, you might ask some broad and general open-ended questions about teaching.

2. *Focus on central ideas.* As the individual begins to tell her story, "Pay close attention to the facts and listen carefully to what is said. Good information is available if you will listen for it" (a chair in the health sciences in a doctoral-granting school). Burley-Allen calls this focusing your attention on the speaker's central ideas: picking out the ideas as they are presented, sorting the facts from the principles, the ideas from examples, and the evidence from opinion.

3. *Keep an open mind.* While listening, "Appreciate and tolerate different points of view" (an anthropology chair in a comprehensive college). To Burley-Allen, this means keeping an open mind and asking questions rather than making statements to clarify your understanding of the communication. Chairpersons should "listen rather than come in with a grand plan" (a philosophy chair in a comprehensive college) and "know when to be silent and when to provide input" (a health sciences chair in a doctoral-granting school). "Hold your rebuttal," said Burley-Allen. You may want to consider jotting down points you want to rebut and later phrase these points as questions.

4. *Write down the ideas and later reflect on them.* One final recommendation from a chair in a department of anthropology in a comprehensive college was to: "Listen more. Write it down. Mull it over. Then reflect on what it means." The act of writing down thoughts improves your ability to remember the speaker's major points, according to Burley-Allen. Writing also indicates to the speaker that she is being heard. Your written remarks may consist of key words, phrases, or ideas.

What should you listen for as the faculty member describes her teaching situation? Chairpersons in our study said you should listen for the interests, needs, and aspirations of the faculty member and their perceptions of issues or problems. Since faculty are professionals, chairpersons must recognize and appreciate their aspirations. A chairperson in a theology department in a research university said, "You should try to get a sense of what people's aspirations are -- what their hopes are for the department and for themselves." A chair in a research university reinforced this concept and suggested matching aspirations with opportunities: "One of the primary jobs of the chair is to keep in touch with what every faculty member is doing, and try to provide the opportunities where they're needed."

Far too often a chair may assess needs on a one-time basis, then fail to keep in touch. Needs of faculty change during a professional career. The "excellent" chairperson frequently reviews and interacts with faculty to ensure mutual understanding. If there is disharmony between assignments and faculty needs and interests, individuals will likely be unhappy and dissatisfied.

Finally, the location of a conversation is important because it says a great deal about who is in charge. Most faculty perceive the chairperson's office as a place where the chair is in charge and where directions will be given. An analogy can be drawn to being called to the principal's office in high school. Conversations that take place in the faculty member's office help professors feel comfortable to speak openly.

A philosophy department chairperson gave this advice: "A chair is not going to be effective if he has to pull the faculty over to the chair's turf. The chair has to enter the faculty members' turf." A research university chair told us: "You have to get into their offices. Talk with them. Ask questions and listen. You can't just do it at annual evaluation time." A chair at a comprehensive college in a large science department suggested: "I spend one hour with every faculty member in their own office each week -- on their own turf -- where they feel at ease." Spending one hour with each individual may consume too much time; some individuals commented that daily contact for shorter periods worked well. But the clear recommendation was for continuing contact with faculty in their own offices or a neutral zone where they could feel comfortable.[2]

Collaboratively set goals.

Assisting faculty in setting professional goals can be a rewarding experience for both you and the faculty member. It is a close interaction that requires care in approach. By listening closely, chairpersons can gain an understanding of each faculty member's concerns, needs and aspirations. A diagnostic step is needed initially to determine how best to relate individual goals to the departmental and institutional mission.

It is important to avoid making assumptions about faculty needs. A chair in political science made the following recommendation:

> I sit down with each faculty member individually and have extended conversations with them about how they feel about the department, their role within the department, and their goals, both short- and long-range. Then I work out in my own mind and write down two or three things that I want to do for each member of the department to improve their morale, solve some problem, or remove some irritant they have identified as an obstacle.

> You don't want to make assumptions about what colleagues want for their professional growth and development. You want to find out from them what they perceive their needs to be. Only after you have a clear, concise sense of what their concerns are, should you set about trying to assist them.

It's important to set realistic goals. If the faculty member has not been very productive, you can't expect miracles overnight. A chairperson in a language/literature department indicated:

> I help faculty develop clear, concise, realistic goals with a timeline for accomplishing them. You have to be realistic. You can't expect a person who hasn't done much for five years to suddenly bloom into something outstanding.

---

[2] In their popular book, *In Search of Excellence*, Peters and Waterman call this "Management by Wandering Around" (1984, p. 260).

Help faculty set priorities for use of their professional time. Faculty may be reluctant to say "no" to the wide range of opportunities. An English chair in a small selective liberal arts college talked about helping his colleagues say "no":

> A general approach to encouraging or helping my colleagues is to teach them how to say "no" to some very convincing appeals. The chair does, I think, have the moral obligation to take courage, look at his or her colleagues -- look them in the face at the end of the year and say, "From my vantage point, however limited it may be, it seems to me you're doing too much of *X* and not enough of *Y*." Just confess the weakness of the information -- "I may not have much to work on. I'm not coming down heavy. I'm not an authority. You know how little power I have. But this is the way I perceive it, and maybe others are perceiving it this way also."

Collaboratively setting goals with faculty involves visiting with them to diagnose their needs, linking individual goals to the departmental goals and institutional mission, checking to make sure that individual plans are realistic, and then helping faculty members say "no" to peripheral involvements so they can realize their goals.

Provide feedback to faculty.

Department chairpersons must provide feedback to faculty members regardless of whether performance is positive or needs improvement. Providing this kind of feedback requires the utmost in interpersonal skills. A chair in political science from a doctoral-granting school said:

> There is a tendency to give up on certain people. If you have somebody in his late fifties or sixties who hasn't done anything professionally and seems to be teaching from those old yellowed pages, there is a tendency to ignore that person and work around him. You really shouldn't neglect him.

Acknowledging that not all people can be helped, "excellent" chairs nevertheless stressed becoming involved with faculty and confronting them when necessary. The faculty member may not realize there is a problem. A chair in the hard sciences said, "I visited with her about the student's complaints. At first she seemed shocked that there was a problem." A chair in another institution advised, "Start easy. The person needs a friend. Work on it together."

Lawrence Brammer, a noted authority on interpersonal skills, discusses seven techniques useful in confronting individuals (1979, pp. 86-88):

1. Give observations in the form of feedback when individuals are ready.

2. Describe the behavior before giving your reaction to it.

3. Give feedback about the behavior rather than judgments about the person.

4. Give feedback about things that the person has the capacity to change.

5. Give feedback in small amounts so that the individual can experience the full impact of your reaction.

6. Give prompt feedback to current and specific behavior, not unfinished emotional business from the past.

7. Later, ask the individual for reactions to your feedback. Did it enhance the relationship or diminish it?

Using feedback steps such as Brammer's, recognizing that faculty may not be aware of a problem, and confronting faculty when the situation merits it allows chairs to challenge individuals without diminishing their dignity and self-esteem.

Represent faculty to colleagues and senior administrators.

Building positive relationships can be enhanced by chairs advocating for an individual faculty member with senior colleagues or administrators on campus. A psychology chairperson in a doctoral-granting school discussed this role:

I have to say the only crucial thing is to be on the faculty's side. You have to be their advocate. You also must be your staff person's advocate. Chairs or faculty can't offend secretaries and still hope to get things done.

A chair in a department of psychology in a doctoral-granting institution reinforced the concept of protection:

> I think it is very important that the department head establish the mental set within the department that the head is the departmental advocate. If the faculty don't perceive you as their advocate, you have a very tough row to hoe.

The chairperson is typically a "buffer" between faculty and upper-level administration. A genetics chair in a research university talked about his role as a "buffer":

> The most important thing I can do is be a buffer between the faculty and the administration. I also try to keep the administrative responsibilities of the faculty to an absolute minimum so the faculty can focus their time on teaching and research.

What does "buffering" mean? For one individual it meant "taking the heat" from upper-level administration. A liberal arts college chair discussed this situation:

> The chair has to be willing to incur the wrath of higher administration. The chair's position is to argue as effectively as possible for the concerns of the faculty and the department. The chair needs to be the faculty voice to the administration.

The chair may indeed be the only voice faculty have with administration; it is understandable, then, that faculty feel strongly about the chair's advocacy role. Walking the tightrope between being an advocate for faculty and supportive of the administration offers the department chair a unique challenge.

Serve as a role model and mentor.

One strategy used by chairpersons to gain confidence of upper-level administrators as well as departmental faculty is to model high levels of performance and to mentor faculty toward attaining high levels of performance in their own right. Chairpersons who stressed the concept of role modeling described setting a good example for faculty:

> It's extremely important that the chair serve as a role model. Don't expect of others what you won't do yourself. For example, if there is a big concern about professional growth and development within a department, you shouldn't be the chairperson if you can't set the pace in that area [a chairperson in political science in a doctoral-granting school].

Try to set a good example for the faculty in teaching, research, and faculty development in general. Get good marks in those areas yourself and it's impact carries over to your department, the institution, and off-campus [a chairperson in sociology/ anthropology in a comprehensive college].

The first thing I would do is model the behavior that I expect from others. If you want them to be productive and to participate in activities, you have to model that yourself. But you have to try to maintain some stability, working at a balance [a chairperson in special education in a research university].

Although you can model levels of high performance for faculty in departments, it is wise to respect individual differences in people. A chairperson commented: "Don't try to clone yourself—different people accomplish goals in different ways." System theorists speak of the concept "equifinality," the notion that there are many ways to achieve objectives. Likewise, people approach their jobs differently. Individuality was underscored by an English chair in a liberal arts school:

Each person is an individual. The chair needs to be attentive to what each person thinks is important. We have several faculty members who are extremely individualistic. They have their own beliefs and their own ideas. They don't want to be molded by any means. The chair has to acknowledge individual differences and use them so the faculty member grows.

Look to senior faculty as role models and mentors for junior faculty. "Lighten your load," said one chairperson. This advice is especially appropriate in a large department where it may be impossible to spend adequate time with all faculty. The satisfaction gained by an older faculty member assisting a younger individual can be salutary for both parties involved. A dance and drama chair reflected on the influence a senior faculty had on her career:

The trend I see with most of the faculty is that the younger faculty look more to senior faculty for values, leadership, and encouragement. Senior professors as mentors, have some responsibility for the development of younger staff. When I joined this faculty without much experience, there were senior faculty who were extremely helpful, encouraging, and responsible for me. I am very grateful to them.

Chairs need to keep standards for themselves that they hold for faculty, respect individual differences in faculty members, and encourage senior members in the department to serve as role models and mentors for junior faculty.

Encourage and support faculty.

To help faculty reach high levels of performance, cultivate their individual strengths and encourage them in the areas in which they excel. A psychology chair in a liberal arts school combined assessing faculty strengths with encouragement:

> Number one, you should concentrate on assessing your faculty's strengths and weaknesses. Two, encourage, encourage, encourage. Play upon those strengths and almost ignore or minimize the weaknesses. Don't hone in on the weaknesses. As an administrator, you can bring a positive perspective that others may not see.

This statement reinforces the message of an old song, "You've got to accentuate the positive and eliminate the negative." Chairs sometimes concentrate on individual weaknesses and ignore strengths. "Understand where faculty strengths are rather than trying to change faculty," said a computer science chair in a research university. He continued,

> Certainly people have hidden strengths that one can bring out. It takes a while to understand what makes people enthusiastic and put in extra effort. Not all faculty can get national research reputations, although we push that as much as possible. Sometimes it's important to find other vehicles. For example, one faculty member is good with people and administration; another is a prolific writer of books; another is an excellent teacher; another loves to make computer systems and is now responsible for early training of graduate students in systems development.

In educational circles, the idea being discussed here is known as "differentiated staffing" -- to assign and encourage faculty in areas in which they excel; not to expect all faculty to engage in the same activities.

There is no set pattern for support and encouragement. The chairperson of a health sciences department in a research university indicated that it is important to "follow your instincts about encouraging people to be their best." Another individual used positive reinforcement and feedback:

> You have to allow faculty to make a little progress at a time and keep encouraging them. Use positive reinforcement all the

> time, constant input and feedback [a chairperson in languages
> and literature in a doctoral-granting school].

The effective chairs recognized the need to encourage all faculty. It is easy to give up, especially when there is little indication of an individual's progress or interest in trying to improve.

> Don't neglect the ones that seem to be doing fine; give them
> encouragement. Also, though it sounds preachy, don't give up
> on anybody. My own sense is that the "deadwood" has gotten
> that way largely because they have been neglected. You should
> keep trying to know individuals in terms of their own aspirations
> and hopes for the department. There is often some way to
> rekindle some spark within them [a chairperson in computer
> science].

This advice may sound simple or easy. It is not. It is a challenge to identify strengths or an area of interest where the faculty member is willing to invest time and energy. "It's not always easy to find where initiative lies in a faculty member," said a philosophy chairperson in a research university. "At the same time you encourage initiative, it must be done with restraint and respect. I've seen quite a few chairs work at encouraging initiative but some are overbearing."

Work hard to identify the strengths of the faculty, build on these strengths through encouragement, and work with all faculty -- the producers and the non-producers alike. When change does occur, be ready to provide encouragement and reinforcement.

Suggested Resources

Books

Bolton, R. *People Skills: How to Assert Yourself, Listen to Others, and Resolve Conflicts.* New York: A Touchstone Book, Simon & Schuster, Inc., 1979.

Robert Bolton writes about communication skills. He gives a detailed analysis of conflict management skills useful in confronting and providing feedback to individuals. The book is largely a "self-help" document, with exercises to be completed by the reader. The description of the helping process and discussion of the helper's role are especially useful.

Brammer, L. *The Helping Relationship: Process and Skills.* (2nd ed.) Englewood Cliffs, New Jersey: Prentice-Hall, Inc.,1979.

Lawrence Brammer's writing is intended for people who wish to help "normal individuals to function at a higher level." Brammer asserts that listening is a passive act, used by the helper, to understand the content of another's communication. "Listening with the third ear" requires a listener to be silent most of the time, while allowing another person to talk. This involves attending, paraphrasing, clarifying, perception checking, indirect leading, direct leading, and questioning skills. Brammer also discusses micro-counseling skills such as reflecting, confronting, and informing.

Burley-Allen, M. *Listening: The Forgotten Skill.* New York: John Wiley and Sons, Inc., 1982.

Madelyn Burley-Allen's discusses "active listening" and how to do it. This book is based on her 10 years of experience teaching seminars on the subject and requests from the participants. The importance and power of effective listening are discussed. The book details methods for improving personal listening capabilities. Skills included in her book but not mentioned in this chapter are observing nonverbal cues, summarizing, evaluating, and criticizing content (not the speaker's delivery). We recommend her self-assessment tools and numerous examples about effective listening.

Fisher, R., and Ury, W. *Getting to Yes: Negotiating Agreement without Giving In.* New York: Penguin Books, 1981.

Roger Fisher and William Ury provide four considerations to facilitate success when using "win-win" negotiation methods: separate the people from the problem; focus on interests, not positions; generate a variety of possibilities before deciding what to do; and insist that the result be based on some objective standard.

Kouzes, J.M., and Posner, B.Z. *The Leadership Challenge: How to Get Extraordinary Things Done in Organizations.* San Francisco: Jossey-Bass, 1988.

This book was also referred to in the "Suggested Resources" section for Chapter Three. The concise discussion about trust and openness in Kouzes and Posner's book is commendable (Part 4). The authors consider the importance of building trusting relationships and the impact of trust on open communication in a section on "fostering collaboration."

Part II

Applying the Strategies

CHAPTER FIVE

Help Newly-Hired Faculty Become Adjusted and Oriented

All new faculty need assistance; I just take that as a given. It's not hard to see young academic people struggling with priorities. They ask, "What's the most important use of my time?" It is one of the toughest questions we deal with, and it has to be dealt with directly [a chemistry chairperson in a doctoral-granting school].

My job is to bring together the package of resources that will provide the physical and financial environment that allows new faculty to flourish [a biology chairperson in a major research university].

As the present faculty work force ages, selects early retirement, or reaches mandatory retirement age in the next decade, an increasing number of new faculty will be joining academic departments. These new staff will need to establish a sense of identity, ownership, and belonging in the department. They may be recent graduates assuming their first teaching posts, experienced faculty moving from another institution, or temporary or part-time staff promoted to full-time positions.

What are the needs and expectations of individuals during the first year or two of their careers in a new academic department? All faculty experience predictable phases of settling in, adjusting, and carving out niches in academic units. You might reflect on your own early experiences as a new member of the department. This reflection may provide valuable insight about what to do and what to avoid when working with new staff.

This chapter advances a four-step approach for helping faculty adjust to the department:

1. Make a personal commitment to help the new faculty member and convey this commitment to the individual.

2. Discuss with the individual his or her needs and expectations.

3. Discuss and help establish a supportive work environment for the individual.

4. Look for tangible signs of success and reinforce them.

Make a personal commitment to help the new faculty member.

A personal commitment to help a newly-hired faculty member is a result of several factors. Since chairs are often involved in the hiring process, they hold a personal stake in the long-term career of the individual. As a history chair in a comprehensive college said, "I felt a special responsibility for new faculty coming into the department." Chairs also hold a professional responsibility to the academic unit. As another chair commented, "The higher the quality of the faculty, the better the department."

A personal commitment from the chair may be conveyed to the new faculty member during the job interview or within the first year. A government chairperson in a doctoral-granting school said that she "counseled with [new faculty members] before [they] arrived on campus." By deciding to help newly-hired faculty and by conveying that commitment to them personally, the chairperson begins a support system that will ensure that the individual has a sense of longevity in the department.

Discuss individual needs and expectations.

Visit with new faculty members to determine what they will need to succeed and what you, the department, and the institution expect of them.[3] Also, recognize that faculty may not be aware of what they need. This point was conveyed best by a chairperson in the hard sciences in a major research university:

> We ask [beginning faculty] for a very definite list of their needs.
> But you have to realize that we also know, perhaps better than
> they, what they're going to need. It's coaching them to what
> they really need. We have a very good idea of what it's going to
> take for a person's development.

Thus, during an early conversation with a new staff member, find out what they perceive their needs to be. The following rough categorization of potential needs, drawn from the literature about new faculty may be useful to organize your thoughts. Consider needs in six categories:

1. Intellectual companionship;

2. Support and encouragement from colleagues;

---

[3] These needs represent a composite identified in three sources of information discussing characteristics of new professors. (See Fink, 1984, pp. 43-52; Baldwin and Blackburn, 1981, p. 609; and Barber, 1987, p. 40.)

3. Identification with the institution;

4. Knowledge about the formal and information operations of the institution;

5. Knowledge about role expectations of the campus;

6. Released time from a demanding schedule to become oriented and adjusted to a new work situation.

With these needs in mind, you might go to the individual's office and serve as an informal "sounding board." In a small liberal arts college, the chair of a psychology department visited with an individual who had arrived on campus:

> I went into her office and said "How are things going?" "What are you up to?" "What sorts of needs do you have?" With these questions, I hoped to make the person feel wanted and supported.

Giving support to newly-hired faculty also requires a chair to give a clear answer to a common faculty question, "What do I need to do in order to succeed here?" In a research study where tenured faculty at a major midwestern university were asked about their early career stages, two-thirds commented that performance expectations were neither explicit nor clear during their first years on campus (Corcoran and Clark, 1984, p. 123). A human resources chair in a doctoral-granting school spoke about discussing "expectations":

> The challenge for one new faculty member was to remind her that now she was on a tenure track and had a doctorate. There were going to be substantial expectations of her in the area of scholarly activity. I also reminded her that teaching expectations were no less. She had two hats, both of them bigger than the original teaching hat that she came in with.

By visiting with a new faculty member, chairpersons can show "interest and support," help the person get off to a "positive" start, and, as a history chair said, "try to make him (the new member) feel like a regular faculty member."

Establish a supportive environment for the individual.

The next step is to consider how you, as chair, can build a supportive work environment that will enable the individual to succeed in the department and the institution. As you help new faculty, consider the perceptions of senior faculty in your unit. Senior faculty may challenge you with charges of favoritism toward new faculty. "I think there comes a time," said a chairperson in the humanities, "when you have to gamble in terms of bending the university rules and perhaps unfairly allocating departmental resources, unfair in the eyes of some of the faculty." To counteract charges of preferential treatment, "excellent" chairpersons recommended openly discussing the charges with senior faculty, reminding them of what *their* needs were during their first years in a new department. The senior faculty, like chairs, have an investment in the department and therefore also in the new member. "When new faculty are helped," commented a chairperson in the social sciences, "we all benefit in the department. I view my assistance as helping a person succeed in being a productive member of the department, which, in turn, translates into a successful department."

Four approaches can help build a supportive work environment: allocating resources, networking, integrating, and adjusting workloads and assignments.

Allocating Resources. Resources may consist of secretarial assistance, institutional funds for projects, study leaves for graduate school, "seed" money for equipment and laboratories, and information about the department and institution. Each provides a tangible form of support from the department to new faculty.

In the hard sciences and medical sciences especially, one finds the procurement of funds for new faculty a special responsibility of the chairperson. For example, in a medical sciences department, the chairperson struck an "agreement" with an incoming faculty member about resources for his laboratory operation:

> His first semester on board I did not burden him with any classroom teaching so that he had a semester free to set up his laboratory and could concentrate on his writing, grantsmanship, and publications. We provided seed money for chemicals and supplies for his laboratory. He was certainly encouraged to pursue "starter" grants, and I helped him with contacts. And he's been successful in receiving several small grants [of] around $8,000 or $9,000 each.

Information about the institution provided through new staff orientation programs represents another important resource, though an active involvement by chairs in the orientation takes away from other chair duties. New staff may view orientation as another hurdle before forging on with other tasks. However, an orientation helps individuals identify with the institution and learn about the formal operation of the school. It sends a message to faculty that they will be supported and encouraged, and it builds faculty ownership for departmental goals and mission.

Many institutions offer college-wide orientations for new staff. Some are one-day orientations; others span several weeks during the first academic semester or quarter. In small liberal arts colleges, orientation is often informal.

To illustrate the components of an orientation program, an economics chair in a southern university discussed a detailed, two-day program her department offers to new faculty and assistant professors. This orientation program lasts for four to five hours each day. The chairs talk about the university from the faculty point of view. The topics addressed include:

1. Services available for advising students;

2. Use of teaching assistants and research assistants;

3. Responsibilities of the chair;

4. Responsibilities of faculty to the chair, such as completing written course outlines at the beginning of each semester;

5. The drop-and-add process;

6. Grading procedures;

7. Relationship of the department to the dean's office and the services available through the dean's office ("I walk them over to the dean's office and introduce them to the staff");

8. A review of the essential points of the faculty handbook and a discussion about "unprofessional behavior"; and

9. A review of the criteria for tenure and promotion ("Of course, they're always very interested in knowing this!").

In summarizing the experience, the chair commented,

It is a full orientation session. It pays off. They don't remember everything, but it gives them a chance to ask questions and raise issues and to get a feel for the fact that they're going to be supported by their colleagues, their chair, and other personnel.

Departments with a small number of faculty may use other methods for orientation. For example, on small liberal arts college campuses, deans often hold formal programs; and chairs support the deans by informally conveying the collegiate values, traditions, and history of the institution. A chairperson in mathematics described a typical situation:

> Oh, it's standing around in the hallway and over coffee. Our office arrangements are nice in that we're all together: there's a nice wide hallway. We've got a coffee pot, so a lot is communicated informally.

What kinds of information are being communicated? "The nature of the curriculum," said one chair from a small college setting, "because new faculty always need to talk to somebody about what's going on in our freshman course."

Networking. New faculty, especially those in their first teaching post, need help making contacts both on and off campus. They require the intellectual companionship of identifying with faculty with similar interests on campus and off campus (e.g., in state, regional, and national professional associations). One illustration of networking comes from a state college with a strong "outreach" mission.

A chair in art and art education first encouraged a new professor to return to graduate school and obtain a doctorate. Once the professor earned the credential, the chair began networking with state professional organizations. She speaks about this situation:

> Having been here so long, I have many contacts. And I have been on many art committees, and [when they came around for new people] I tried to get this professor on as many of them as possible, especially in the state association. When I stepped aside as president of the association, I appointed him vice-president. Now he is president. By encouraging him to be active in professional organizations, he is now getting a lot of speaking engagements on his own, but initially I gave him contacts.

Visiting with the faculty member involved in this situation confirmed this assistance. "She is always encouraging me, giving me information about jobs, placing me on statewide committees - in short, helping me network."

Integration. Integrating or involving faculty in priority projects within the department helps new staff identify with the institution and establish intellectual companionship. An opportunity for chairs to promote integration occurs when faculty discuss their professional goals with the chair. An economics chairperson in a small department with five faculty at a liberal arts college talked about co-authoring grant proposals, team-teaching courses, and providing resources to improve the skills of a new faculty member. He began by discussing how the faculty in the department "identified areas for the department and the faculty for improvement and change." They developed a long-range plan to incorporate international business, interdisciplinary studies, and the use of computers into their program. When a new faculty member was hired two years ago, the chair visited with the person about his professional goals and together they mapped a plan to include the individual in three departmental priorities:

> In the international business area, I involved him in two grant proposals. He serves as assistant director of one of the grants, specifically one involving seminars and workshops, as well as revising courses and creating new courses. In fact, he decided to create a course in international business. I think it is good for our program and good for the professor.

> Then I persuaded him to participate in an interdisciplinary studies project on critical thinking. He attended seminars and is currently revising a course that emphasizes thinking and higher-order reasoning.

> We have also cooperated with other departments integrating computers into courses. With the help of a small grant, he is exploring the literature in order to do this.

> My feeling is that business professors tend to have a somewhat narrow approach out of their MBA training. So for our liberal arts college setting, an exposure to other disciplines would be most helpful. That's where the projects in international business, critical thinking, and computers come in.

By including this individual in activities, the chair provided an integrating mechanism that fostered identity, ownership, and a sense of belonging.

Adjusting Workloads and Assignments. New faculty need time to become adjusted to a new work environment. Chairpersons can adjust faculty loads or assignments to protect time demands on individuals. In terms of teaching loads, a chairperson in public policy at a comprehensive college limited the number of teaching preparations so that a faculty member could finish her dissertation.

> I've basically given her course assignments that would not require major preparation or new preparations. After the first year, I had her repeating the same courses that she taught in that first year. One thing that I can do as a chair is schedule courses, class times, and advisement assignments so that she has minimal distractions from the dissertation.

L. Dee Fink, in a study of first-year geography professors, corroborates this chair's observation: "It is not the number of classroom hours itself that creates problems for new teachers but the number of class preparations and the number of students involved"(1984, p. 41). Fink suggests three considerations that affect size of a teaching load: aspects of the course itself (e.g., the number of preparations, number of students, number of classroom hours per week, and the nature of the subject matter); the nature of the institution and the department (e.g., graduate student oriented, a strong emphasis on scholarship); and the level of teaching experience of the faculty member.

An illustration of building a supportive work environment.

An example from a biochemistry department at a major research university illustrates the four approaches to establishing a supportive work environment. This department consisted of twenty-three faculty. The university had allocated the department funds to build a "first-rate program" in the life science area. The chair reflected on his role: "A very important part of my work is to foster development of younger colleagues who have a lot of potential." The chair next described his overall plan to help nurture "rising young stars":

> *Resources.* Once we decide to invite a young scholar to join us, it is my job as chairman to bring together the package of resources that will provide this young person with all of the physical and financial environment that allows him or her to flourish. It means securing university dollars for equipment.

Networking. We advise the individual about where to and how to obtain outside funding (after having spent the funds the university can provide).

Integration. We bring the new person into the decision-making process as soon as we can. The newest assistant professor has one vote on most faculty issues just like the full professor.

Assignments and Workloads. We also try not to overburden new faculty. We lighten the teaching loads. We take advantage of their training and expertise. We rotate teaching assignments so that new staff teach undergraduate and graduate courses.

The chairman summarized, "We try to develop an environment where the new teacher-scholar feels membership in a warm and receptive group."

Look for tangible signs of adjustment and orientation.

After making a personal commitment to help a new faculty member, discussing individual needs and expectations, and establishing a positive work environment, look for tangible signs of adjustment and orientation and reinforce them during the pre-tenure or early years of a faculty member's service. Is the individual taking action to meet the needs identified as common to new faculty? Look for signs of growth, such as companionship, support, identification with the school, understanding of the institution and institutional expectations, and time-use skills. For example, signs of successful adjustment include developing new courses, recruiting students, publishing in journals, writing grant proposals, and/ or setting up work laboratories.

Less tangible signs of success include positive attitudes and a sense of satisfaction with the department:

He obviously has to be very satisfied with what he is doing, and I think that satisfaction has been translated into his willingness to stay here and be part of this program [a chair of parks and recreation in a doctoral-granting school].

I think that he has been more than willing to cooperate in the department in research and scholarship. He feels the sense of reward. I think he's moving along very well [a pharmacy chair in a major university].

Signs of productivity and a positive attitude are monitored by chairs throughout the first few years of a new faculty member's career. It represents an important follow-up step for department chairs who want to enhance the work environment for newly-hired faculty.

Suggested Resources

Books and Periodicals

The first two writings examine different aspects of Roger Baldwin's doctoral dissertation through which he developed a five-stage model of professional career development for faculty members at liberal arts institutions.

Baldwin, R. "Adult and Career Development: What Are the Implications
for Faculty." In *Current Issues in Higher Education, 1979.*
Washington D.C.: American Association for Higher Education,
1979.

Baldwin discusses adult developmental theories in relation to faculty members' careers. Asserting that faculty career development is a life-long process, five developmental stages are presented. Stages one and two are concerned with assistant professors in the first and second three-year period of their career. Associate professors are in stage three. Full professors less and more than five years from retirement are those in stages four and five. Baldwin relates these five stages to the stages of adult career development posed by Super, Hall, and Nougaim. The balance of the article contains a discussion of attitudes, needs, career changes, values, and goals related to persons experiencing each stage of Baldwin's model.

Baldwin, R., and Blackburn, R. "The Academic Career as a Developmental
Process." *Journal of Higher Education*, 1981, 52, 598-614.

Roger Baldwin and Robert Blackburn review the faculty development literature and discuss in detail the stable and unstable aspects of faculty careers. They discuss characteristics of individuals in each of the five stages of Baldwin's career model. The characteristics of individuals in the first two stages are most important for the content of Chapter Five in this book.

Baldwin, R., and Others. *Expanding Faculty Options: Career Development Projects at Colleges and Universities.* Washington, D.C.: American Association for Higher Education, 1981.

Roger Baldwin and his colleagues at the American Association for Higher Education studied several faculty development projects on two- and four-year college campuses during the 1980-1981 school year. Specifically, they explored career transition projects for new academics and projects for expanding options of community college faculty members. The writers studied six types of projects with aims related to career development and/or provision of career change assistance.

Burke, D. "The Academic Marketplace in the 1980's: Appointment and Termination of Assistant Professors." *The Review of Higher Education,* 1987, 10, 199-214.

Delores Burke replicated the study by Caplow and McGee cited below. Burke describes results of a study of the academic workplace in relation to its employees. Processes of faculty recruitment into, and separation from, the institution are specifically discussed. Interestingly, the importance of the academic department is seen as stronger in both of those processes than are the influences of administrators above the department level.

Caplow, T., and McGee, R. J. *The Academic Marketplace.* Garden City, New York: Anchor Books, 1965.

This book is a second publication of the authors' 1958 classic on recruitment, selection, and the general hiring process in academia. There is no substitute for the insights offered. The study discussed by the authors was conducted in liberal arts departments at nine universities. The unit of measurement was each full-time faculty vacancy and replacement which occurred during the two-year period of their exploration. Faculty mobility appears to have been the motivation for the study. Reasons and procedures for the research are explained, then a systematic analysis of each stage in the process of having a vacancy created and filled is addressed. Trends and recommendations relevant to the mid-1950's are included. The academic profession is laden with tradition. We recommend this book and the timeless nature of its content.

Cornford, F.M. *Microcosmographia Academica: Being a Guide for The Young Academic Politician.* Chicago: University of Chicago Press, 1922.

Something on the lighter side! Cornford presents a whimsical treatment of getting started as a professor. This little handbook will remind you of your first days on the job. The first chapter title is "Warning" and what an ominous commentary begins there. The chapter begins, "My heart is full of pity for you, O young academic politician." Other chapters are titled "Parties," "Caucuses," "On Acquiring Influence....," "Principles....," "The Political Motive," "Argument," "The Conduct of Business.," "Squaring....," and "Farewell."

Fink, L.D. *The First Year of College Teaching.* New Directions for Teaching and Learning, no. 17. San Francisco: Jossey-Bass, 1984.

L. Dee Fink examines the experiences of one hundred new geography professors in doctoral-granting institutions. He addresses specific issues of concern to new teachers: What prior experiences prepared them for college teaching? What effects did these experiences have on their performance? What situations did they face when they started to teach? What did they try to do as a teacher in a college or university? How well did they perform during their first year? How did they feel about their first year as a full-fledged academic faculty member? And what effect did these feelings have on their future career plans?

Gilligan, C. *In a Different Voice: Psychological Theory and Women's Development.* Cambridge, MA. Harvard University Press, 1982.

Carol Gilligan wrote this book after reviewing developmental theories specifically related to the study of male populations and conducting several research projects. The studies conducted by Gilligan and her associates involved those on abortion decisions, college students, rights and responsibilities, and images of violence. The results of these studies are related to her assertions about psychological development of women. The tendency for women to emphasize relationship with and empathy for others as influences on personal development and success is discussed. Gilligan sees male patterns of development, in which individuation is supported, as a better fit to the demands of employment in the corporate world.

Lazarus. B., and Tolpin, M. "Engaging Junior Faculty in Career Planning: Alternatives to the Exit Interview." In *Current Issues in Higher Education, 1979*. Washington D.C.: American Association for Higher Education, 1979.

Barbara Lazarus and Martha Tolpin offer models of career planning for junior faculty. The impetus for their writing is the condition of limited employment opportunity in the academic setting. Many of the specific programs highlighted are targeted toward female faculty members. Workshops, sponsored by Higher Education Resource Services (HERS), are discussed. Goals of those workshops include learning about women's academic careers, teaching skill development for the academy, and building networks.

Marchese, T. *The Search Committee Handbook: A Guide to Recruiting Administrators*. Washington D.C.: American Association for Higher Education, 1987.

Ted Marchese has compiled a recommended guide to the search process. *The Search Committee Handbook* is designed to assist search committees charged with the responsibility of filling academic administrative positions. The content is applicable to any academic hiring situation. Marchese presents questions to be asked before, during, and after a vacancy is filled. He discusses many facets in the processes of needs analysis, recruitment, and hiring of a replacement. Organized search methods, structure, function, requirements, and documentation of search committee needs are included.

Mathis, B.C. "Academic Careers and Adult Development: A Nexus for Research." In *Current Issues in Higher Education, 1979*. Washington D.C.: American Association for Higher Education, 1979.

B. Claude Mathis discusses a definition of career and the orientation of faculty development to teaching issues. While arguing for a view of faculty development wider than teaching, Mathis describes four periods he views as crucial for administrative and institutional interventions. These periods include graduate school, the early career, mid-to-late career and retirement. Institutional involvement in faculty career development is highlighted most directly in relationship to fostering faculty development policy initiatives.

CHAPTER SIX

Improve the Teaching Performance of Faculty

The inexperienced teacher:
It's easier to encourage someone to become a better scholar than teacher. Most people coming from graduate school with a Ph.D. know about being a scholar. They often have little knowledge about teaching unless they have a "gift" for it. But even the "gift" needs to be shaped with help, advice, and encouragement [a dance and drama chairperson in a liberal arts school].

The experienced teacher:
How do you change the personality of a faculty member who has been teaching for 25 years? [a humanities chair in a small liberal arts college].

A lthough the degree of emphasis faculty and institutions place on teaching, scholarship, and service depends largely on the mission and orientation of each institution, all schools have the common requirement that faculty must be successful teachers to advance in rank and become contributing department members.

On the whole, faculty perform capably as teachers. However, for reasons related to motivation, skills, or the work environment, certain individuals do not perform up to their abilities. While some faculty can improve their teaching without outside help, others need added support and encouragement. Since department chairs often evaluate faculty and provide rewards for good teaching, they can be instrumental in offering assistance to professors.

What forms does this assistance take? In this chapter we advance a five-step process based largely on consultative models available from the field of instructional development.[4]

[4.] We are indebted to authors who helped to shape our understanding of this process: Karron Lewis's seven-step approach (1988, pp. 21-22); Joyce Povlac's five-step Teaching Analysis Program (1988, pp. 82-84); Smith and Schwartz's model for the "reflective practitioner" (1988, pp. 63-85); and Brinko's consultation approach (1988, in press, pp. 3-5).

The steps in this process are:

1. Gather background information;

2. Clarify the problem;

3. Observe performance yourself;

4. Facilitate improvement and practice;

5. Monitor progress and advocate.

Each step will be discussed using illustrations drawn from "excellent" chairs who talked about working through situations with "problem" teachers. After outlining all steps, we will present two illustrations of the process. The process model is based on the assumption that chairs are helping faculty improve their performance, not evaluating current performance. Often the line between development and evaluation is unclear. The process steps focus not only on "what can be done" but also on "how it is done." For us, the process is as important as the specific strategies chairpersons use.

Gather background information.

Before visiting individually with the faculty member about teaching problems, chairpersons should gather information about an individual's performance. All too often chairs rely on student evaluations (e.g., summary scores from student rating forms) as a single source of information about an individual's teaching. Those writing about teaching recommend that multiple sources of information be considered.[5]

Visit with students in your office: "Students were in my office complaining," reported an "excellent" chairperson in music. Talk with senior faculty and administrators. Consider sitting in on meetings called to address problems between students and faculty. By sitting in on such a meeting, one chairperson was able to "forestall and prevent a formal grievance process from being initiated, which, for a new faculty member, could have been quite serious." Visit with other administrators. On smaller campuses, for example, information travels quickly: "There were students commenting to the president and the dean before I heard about the complaints," said one chairperson. Form your own opinion, using

---

[5] The use of multiple approaches, according to O'Hanlon and Mortensen (1980, pp. 664-672), increases the overall fairness of the review and overcomes limitations of any one method.

summary ratings from students' evaluations and by visiting with students and colleagues.

Look for behavioral signs of problems. The signs may be on the faces of individuals or in their voices as they mention their concerns. "I noticed that he was flustered and found it very difficult to teach. He brought this concern to me," said an English chairperson from a selective liberal arts college. The signs may be even more overt, as in the case of the faculty member who "would frequently tape a sign on the door that said: 'No class today.'"

Clarify goals and objectives.

After gathering information about a potential teaching problem, visit with the faculty member formally (e.g., a scheduled meeting in his office) at the earliest possible opportunity. If a semi-annual or annual performance review is due, set aside time during this review to talk about the growth and development of the faculty member as a teacher. For example, in a research university department with eighteen faculty, the fine arts chairperson interviewed all faculty members every semester, giving them an opportunity to "present their concerns to me (and giving me one to present my concerns to them)." A business chair in a comprehensive college met with faculty at the beginning of the academic year. In this interview, the faculty member shared two personal and professional goals, and the chair did the same. In this way, they shared and agreed upon goals for the year. Both beginning-of-the-year and year-end sessions provide an opportunity to explore and clarify teaching problems with faculty.

Karron Lewis (1988, p. 21) calls this phase "conducting a pre-observation interview." What should be considered during this meeting? First, review how the faculty member feels about courses, students, teaching, and causes of the potential problem:

1. Ask for a description of his or her class(es) -- verbal as well as the written syllabus for the course;

2. Listen for the clues to the specific types of feedback the faculty member is seeking or needs (e.g., are my lectures organized? Am I responding adequately to students' questions?);

3. Pay attention to comments that reflect the faculty member's attitude toward students and teaching;

4. Ask if there are any personal factors which may be affecting his or her professional activities (e.g., a new baby or over-commitment on committees).

Second, attempt to discern the issues involved, taking into consideration the experience level of the faculty member in question. "Excellent" chairs mentioned that the problems of inexperienced teachers (pre-tenure cases) related to adjusting to students and the classroom setting and learning the student evaluation procedure. For example, the problems of inexperienced teachers included:

1. Inadequate speaking and communication skills in the classroom;

2. Unfair grading practices;

3. More interest in research than in teaching and students;

4. Inability to relate appropriately to the level of knowledge of students;

5. Unfamiliarity with administering student evaluation forms and interpreting results from them.

For experienced teachers (post-tenure), the problems often arose from in-class situations, such as:

1. Dry, unstimulating lecture methods or a "drab" personality;

2. An arrogant, condescending approach to communication with students;

3. Lack of updated materials and research in classroom content;

4. Inconsistent and disorganized instructional practices such as changing times when tests are given, changing assignments, and not paying attention to the syllabus.

Third, find out how the individual sees the situation. Some may not be aware of a problem; others may be suffering through a painful experience. Regardless of the case, finding out how individuals view the situation can clarify the problem and demonstrate respect for their views. Use good interpersonal skills such as listening and feedback skills introduced in Chapter Four. "Don't be afraid to confront the individual," said one chairperson in our study. "Realize that he may not be aware of the problem, especially in the case of senior, experienced faculty."

This point was brought home in an illustration about a disorganized teacher -- a 45-year-old tenured faculty member in humanities in a liberal arts institution who continually changed assignments, requirements, and test dates. After students complained, the chair visited with her:

At first she seemed shocked that there was a problem. She wasn't aware of it. After the shock wore off, she seemed resentful for a while and avoided me whenever she could.

In approaching a case such as this, the chair might follow these steps:

1. Start easy; she needs a friend. Work on it together and talk in a nonthreatening way.

2. Explore with her the specific source of her disorganization. Why is she disorganized?

3. Suggest alternatives to her that will present new challenges. Help her find developmental grant money.

4. Consider team-teaching with her or assign someone who would be willing to team-teach with her.

5. Refer her to a faculty development program or center if one exists on campus.

Observe the performance yourself.

Your objective at this point is to explore further the potential "problem" of the individual so that an appropriate improvement plan can be developed.

Consider observing the individual's teaching in class. This observation, called a "peer review," has drawn criticism as well as praise from many commentators. The trend, however, seems to be in support of its use. Russell Edgerton, president of the American Association for Higher Education, was quoted ("Higher Education Reformers...," 1988, p. 1) as saying, "We must move to a culture in which peer review of teaching is as common as peer review of research."

One faculty member had trouble as a teacher because he spoke above the knowledge level of the students. A chairperson in biology talked about visiting this individual's classroom:

I sat in on his class and tried to analyze what the problem might be and later tried to point out difficulties he experienced in conveying information from a basic, lower level of understanding to more complex thoughts. We talked about the thought process of a poorly prepared student.

As this quote indicates, the chair visited with the individual about areas of difficulty after observing his classroom performance.

Observing performance will be more objective and may be less obtrusive through use of videotape. A chemistry chairperson in a small liberal arts college described the use of videotaping as a vehicle for sharing information about good teaching techniques.

> We set up a program where he would videotape his lectures and I would videotape my lectures, and we would talk about what I was doing and what he was doing. It was a mechanism to see himself.

Taylor-Way (1988) recommends a videotape recall method for improving teaching. A teacher videotapes the first twenty minutes of a class. The consultant (the chair in our case) reviews the tape with the faculty member within twenty-four hours while the teacher's memory of the class is reasonably fresh. The videotape is interrupted periodically for the teacher to discuss how she or he feels, thinks and acts in teaching during the segment. Then the consultant uses a three-step process:

> 1. Focus on a specific, discrete pattern or regularity where there is a discrepancy between what the teacher sees on the videotape and a more preferred approach.
>
> 2. Give a name to that pattern or regularity.
>
> 3. Reframe or develop with the teacher a strategy or principle of how to reduce the discrepancy. The objective here is to encourage the teacher to add to their repertoire of options.

Facilitate improvement and the practice of new skills.

Work with the individual to develop a plan for improvement. This plan may evolve from sharing information about teaching tips found in books, articles, and workshops. "We have a large bulletin board in the hall," said one chairperson, "where I post notices about upcoming seminars or campus activities that relate to teaching." Refer "problem" teachers to development committees or instructional development centers for assistance. Centers, for example, offer assistance in many areas, including diagnosing problems and observing classroom techniques. A chairperson in accounting at a research university routinely referred inexperienced faculty to such a center. He explained:

> I visited with a junior faculty member and pointed out certain teaching problems. This person was shocked that teaching evaluations were not up to the level he had received at another institution. I suggested he get in touch with the campus office

of instructional development. People from that office came over, talked with him, went to his class, and they videotaped one of his classes. Also, they helped him rework the way he prepared for class and how he conducted the class. As a result, he felt much better about his teaching.

Chairs may provide more experienced faculty material useful for course content. A tenured faculty member in a life sciences department for sixteen years is a "willing soul; she is willing to pitch in and do whatever is asked her, and she has a deep commitment to the department." But she had problems delivering clear instructions to students, planning for instruction, and including current research in her courses. She had attended as many as ten professional conferences but did not seem to apply that information in her classes. The chairperson described the assistance provided:

> I made available to her some literature in her subject field by subscribing to journals that were not in our library. These journals would come directly to her. In addition, I have had several individual conferences with her and we have talked about ways to include current research in lectures.

The chairperson need not be solely responsible for sharing information. A business college in a major research university used outside experts to assist one faculty member in keeping current and credible in an area "where the content and technology were moving so fast that faculty just couldn't keep up." The college brought in outside people from business and industry to address current topics. This outside expertise added credibility to the faculty member's class, and the professor learned a lot about activities in the field.

Practicing elements of good teaching is an important step towards improvement. "Excellent" chairs served as mentors for faculty and role-modeled good teaching behaviors with faculty. For example, a chairperson in English in a liberal arts college recommended to an inexperienced teacher that he attend the chairperson's class as well as the class of a senior faculty member:

> My assistance involved a number of long conversations, and I invited him to sit in on my own classes. At least one other senior member has had him sit in on his classes as well. I should add that this man has been reappointed, and while his problems have not been resolved in the classroom, I think he's certainly improved a great deal and that he feels that the department is on his side.

Chairs can also share their approaches through a team-teaching situation or working directly with the faculty member on the development of course syllabi or course content.

Monitor progress toward improvement and advocate for the individual.

At this point in the process, you begin to cycle back to the first step of gathering information, only this time you review materials and information about a specific problem or issue to determine whether the individual is making progress. This monitoring process takes time: reviewing semester and annual student evaluation forms, visiting with students, and learning from colleagues as well as the individual faculty member.

Once improvement occurs, consider your role as that of an advocate for the individual with those responsible on campus for evaluating and assessing performance. A chair in a liberal arts school talked about this step:

> After the person's work began to show some signs of improvement,
> I told members of the evaluation committee and other members
> in the department to spread the good word that he was trying to
> improve his teaching and we had evidence in hand.

This only works if you honestly and sincerely believe that the individual's performance is improving. It means taking a risk. You cannot know beforehand whether your faculty will improve sufficiently to be promoted, tenured, or meet another's expectations for performance. It also means having to deal with one's own feelings of potential failure and recognizing that you can only *try* to help someone in your department.

Illustrations of the Process

We will illustrate the process of improving teaching performance with two specific cases. Both are drawn from small liberal arts colleges where major emphasis is placed on good teaching. The first situation involved a new, untenured professor who joined the staff in the education department. This individual possessed excellent writing and research skills, but she needed to improve her teaching. "She was a sit-down teacher," and "she had difficulty conveying information students could relate to."
The chairperson described the following steps:

> 1. *Gathering background information.* During the first year the
> chair "just spent time sitting in her office, talking to her, and not
> doing much." But, the chair went on to say he visited with

students about complaints and reviewed carefully the students evaluations.

2. *Clarify the problem.* By the end of the second year, it was necessary to begin taking steps to improve the individual's teaching. The chair and the faculty member visited and began thinking about a "faculty development plan." Several activities were carried out under this plan.

3. *Observe performance yourself.* The chair videotaped the faculty member's teaching in a couple of classes and then reviewed with the individual the strengths and weaknesses of her teaching. Together, they isolated teaching behaviors that needed improvement. Then, the chair sat in on a couple of her classes to observe her.

4. *Facilitating improvement and practice.* They team-taught a course together. This class required that both the chair and the faculty member attend every session. Finally, the dean provided a summer faculty development grant so that the chair and the faculty member could spend three weeks during the summer modifying one of her courses.

5. *Monitoring progress.* Over a period of several years, the chair monitored student evaluations. By the sixth year, teaching had improved: "she had gone from approximately a 1.5 on a 5-point scale (5 as a high point) to a 4.1 or 4.2 in the intervening years." At the end of her sixth year, she was given tenure.

The second case involved a tenured faculty member in the area of speech at a small liberal arts college. This person was an assistant professor who wanted to be promoted to associate professor. Five years earlier the faculty member had gone up for promotion and it was denied; now, he wrote to the chair requesting that his credentials be reviewed once again. What did the chair do?

1. *Gathering background information.* He went to the faculty member to get his permission to study the recommendations of five years earlier. ("I'm reluctant to tell people what to do unless the situation calls for it and they will welcome such help.") Then he talked with each member of the department to compile a description of what the individual should do to improve his teaching.

2. *Clarifying the problem.* Next he visited with the faculty member about what needed to be done. (I asked, "What kind of response from students do you want? Are you interested in finding out what you need to do to improve?")

3. *Observing performance.* The chair suggested that senior faculty members attend the individual's classes and make suggestions for improvement. ("You've just got to ease the person along. See what you can do.")

4. *Advocating.* While the individual worked on improving his teaching, the chair told the provost the person "is working on his teaching." The chair also told members of the promotion committee about the person's progress.

Suggested Resources

Newsletters

The Teaching Professor, (published monthly since 1987 by Magna Publications, Madison, Wisconsin).

This newsletter contains many useful tips and principles about college teaching.

Periodicals

Chronicle of Higher Education. (October 29, 1986) "Recommended Guides for the Beginning Teacher" p. 11.

This is a list of recommended books on teaching in higher education. Three cited in this chapter deserve special mention: Lowman, *Mastering the Techniques of Teaching,* McKeachie, *Teaching Tips: A Guidebook for the Beginning Teacher*, and Noonan (ed.) *Learning About Teaching.*

Books

Lowman, J. *Mastering the Techniques of Teaching.* San Francisco: Jossey-Bass, 1984.

Joseph Lowman's first chapter contains three tables summarizing various aspects of excellent teaching. Chapter Two is directed toward the teacher's ability or inability to present him/herself to a class and the impact of that self-presentation. The emphasis of Chapter Three is on interpersonal aspects of teaching. Chapters Four through Nine contain descriptions of widely ranging classroom teaching and learning techniques. The author concludes by examining good teaching as art, craft, and a personally satisfying goal.

McKeachie, W.T. *Teaching Tips: A Guidebook for the Beginning College Teacher.* Lexington, Massachusetts: D.C. Heath and Company, 1986.

Bill McKeachie's book is now in its eighth edition. This work has become a classic in the field. The author offers a practical, methodical approach to academic course development and conduct. He addresses topics including course development, using discussion methods, lecturing, testing, grading, and specialized issues such as teaching large classes. Teaching techniques, models, and methods are examined. Appendices A and B, respectively, contain a model course evaluation format and a checklist of teaching techniques related to intended outcome goals. The reference list is extensive.

Noonan, J.F. (ed.). *Learning about Teaching.* New Directions for Teaching and Learning, no. 4. San Francisco: Jossey-Bass, 1980.

John Noonan's edited work contains nine perspectives on teaching. Most are personal accounts of the effects of teaching on the teacher/writer, rather than on the students. A notable exception is an article on mentoring students. The writings emphasize teacher involvement in the classroom and the development of good teaching.

Lewis. K., and Povlacs, J. *Face to Face: A Sourcebook of Individual Consultation Techniques for Faculty/Instructional Developers.* Stillwater, Oklahoma: New Forums Press, Inc., 1988.

Chairpersons can learn techniques in one-on-one consultative practice from instructional/faculty development leaders who engage in this process and are writing about it. Karron Lewis and Joyce Povlacs offer a collection of twelve writings dealing with consulting as a faculty development activity. Various authors discuss research related to individual consulting. Other writers discuss individual teaching consultation, individual career development consultation, and individual writing consultation.

CHAPTER SEVEN

Improve the Scholarship of Faculty

T hough research has long been rewarded and emphasized at major research universities, publications and scholarly work are finding a more central role in the working lives of faculty on state college and liberal arts campuses. In light of this fact, faculty need to perform capably on all college campuses as scholars as well as teachers.

Early in their careers, faculty initiate, maintain, and focus on a line of scholarly inquiry. When this fails to happen, especially by the third or fourth year, they jeopardize chances of being promoted or tenured. When tenured faculty have inadequate research portfolios, they risk a negative review for promotion to full professor or become perceived as noncontributing members in departments. Some tenured faculty hired years ago as teachers, not researchers, need to reallocate efforts into scholarly activities, learn the skills of a researcher, and engage in a modicum of scholarly work.

> I don't believe there is a faculty member who doesn't want to be productive. Everyone wants to be. I don't believe there is a faculty member who can't be productive as long as you can find an area where he or she can contribute [an agricultural chairperson in a research university].

> I think they were at a plateau. All they needed was a little spark. I think I know their potential. And I've devised that little spark they needed to get them actively involved in research [a physical education chairperson in a regional university].

When faced with "problem" faculty who need to improve their research performance, how can chairpersons assist? In this chapter we advance a four-step model based on interviews with "excellent" chairs who spoke about improving the scholarly research of their faculty:

1. Detect a problem situation as early as possibly by having a review process in place.

2. Once you detect a problem, visit with the individual to clarify the nature of and reasons for it.

3. Identify a plan for improvement that incorporates strategies within your control.

4. After a suitable period of time, follow up on the plan to see if it has had a positive impact on the individual's behavior; if so, advocate for the individual with faculty and administrators.

Detecting a problem situation as early as possible.

A performance discrepancy, according to Robert Mager and Peter Pipe (1970, p. 7) is a difference between "someone's actual performance and his (or her) desired performance." Feedback about performance discrepancies may come from promotion and tenure committee members, faculty colleagues, or students, administrators, or your own subjective assessment of the situation.

The potential problem should be detected as early as possible. This means a careful review of performance for untenured faculty by at least their third year, well in advance of their tenure review. As a communications chair in a doctoral-granting school said, "It's important to catch problems early because it's impossible to help someone in their fourth or fifth year." For tenured faculty, a process of annual review is helpful because research performance can wax and wane during a career. As mentioned in Chapter Three, a faculty performance information system in the department is a useful mechanism for monitoring faculty output.

Annual performance reviews have become a well-accepted procedure on college campuses. These reviews, conducted at the conclusion of an academic year, provide an opportunity for chairs to annually assess the research productivity of their faculty. Richard Miller, a well-known writer on faculty evaluation procedures, talks about an Annual Academic Performance Review (AAPR):

> This review, involving the chairperson and each faculty member, may be undertaken in the spring. The purpose of this forty-five- to sixty-minute scheduled meeting should be to review the past academic year's activities, to discuss its good and not-so-good aspects, to talk about plans for the coming year, and to consider ways in which chairperson and instructor together can improve the department. The AAPR requires careful preparation, documentation, and written follow-up. All of these take time; but if people are a high institutional priority, the time is well spent [1987, p. 29].

A more elaborate model might include a modified management-by-objective approach whereby goals, mutually agreed upon by the chair and faculty member and specified at the beginning of the academic year, are compared with the accomplishments at the end of the year. Faculty might organize information for the chair to review prior to the meeting. The level and type of detailed documentation required in this review will vary. It may include:

> *Quantitative measures:* such as number of papers presented at conferences, journal articles published, books written, grant proposals authored or funded, and creative performances given.

> *Qualitative measures:* such as citations to published works, articles in high-quality journals, success rate of proposals for research support, attendance at performances, or positive reviews of performances.

> *Peer judgments:* such as letters of support by peers on campus and off campus, and department chair and dean comments.

> *Eminence measures:* such as editorial board appointments to journals, awards for research from professional organizations, invited papers, or requested performances.

> *Self-evaluations:* such as personal statements about performance.[6]

In addition to this documentation, faculty might be asked to answer a set of questions: What impact has their scholarly work had on individuals and groups off campus? What thread of continuity exists among the works? What resources are needed to better conduct scholarly work? How is the work original or unique? What is the individual's plan for continued growth as a researcher?

Annual "activity reports" of scholarly performance can be promoted by chairs in a unit. One such report became a mechanism for motivating senior faculty in a philosophy department. A specially-appointed faculty performance committee in this department collected research data from faculty and organized it into a report. This report contained information about faculty accomplishments during the year and anticipated accomplishments during the next year. In the process of compiling the report, the committee resolved difficult questions such

---

[6] This list is adapted from a table of measures of research productivity reported by Creswell (1985, p. 54).

as: What are the major areas of research productivity? How do we weigh them? How do we determine that one person's performance is better than another's? "As a result," commented the chair, "the faculty get to see a cross-section of all of their colleagues. It heightens their awareness of their own productivity, and it encourages them to plan."

An informal review system may work equally well. Chairpersons can visit informally with faculty about their performance, asking them about progress, new ventures, and their hopes for publications. This practice seems to work with senior faculty, as a computer science chair in a major research university commented: "He'd come in and I would say, 'How's it going? How is your book coming along?' You know, it's all those little things."

Clarify the reasons for lack of performance.

Explore with the faculty member the nature of the problem and the reasons for it. Keep in mind the importance of the process; be mindful of good listening skills and appropriate feedback approaches mentioned in Chapter Four of this book. For example, make the individual feel comfortable (an active listening skill) and give feedback when the individual is ready for it (a feedback skill). A chair in veterinary science talked about his process:

> It is difficult when you're dealing with criticism and at the same
> time providing total support for an individual. When you visit
> with a person, after you break the ice and introduce the problem
> as you see it, you might say, "Now that probably looks negative
> to you, but it is my responsibility to try to address this situation,
> turn it around, look at the positive side, and see what we can do."

The individual may deny the problem at first or become enraged or angered, similar to the first steps in the grieving or dying process which has been well documented by Elizabeth Kubler-Ross.[7] This initial reaction should give way to acceptance and a willingness to explore or seek options for improving performance.

---

[7] Kubler-Ross (1975, p. 10) discusses the five stages of dying as denial, rage and anger, bargaining, depression, and acceptance.

During these visits, explore the reasons or causes for poor research performance. At least four types of causes surfaced during our interviews, and they illustrate the range of possibilities.[8]

1. *Lack of skills:*

* Lack effective research skills such as computer, writing, library, or method skills.

* Needs to improve skills in a specific scholarly area such as learning to write grant proposals or combining artistic performances with writing.

2. *Lack of motivation and interest:*

* Spends an inordinate amount of time on teaching duties and claims not to have time for research.

*Places virtually all of her time on training students and considers undergraduate teaching and what happens to students after graduation to be the ultimate priorities.

3. *Personal reasons:*

* Lacks patience necessary to revise and improve manuscripts.

* Holds standards so high that all research is imperfect (a clue: manuscripts are labeled "draft").

* Interests keep shifting; person dabbles in many areas, causing unfocused research.

* Takes a rejection notice from a publisher or editorial board as a bitter defeat and vows not to write again.

4. *Obstacles in the work setting:*

* Lacks the equipment necessary to conduct research.

---

[8] We chose to use categorizes representing a modification of causes discussed by Robert Mager and Peter Pipe (1970, pp. 101-104). They suggest that individuals might ask themselves: (1) Is it a skill deficiency? (2) Is the desired performance punishing? (3) Is non-performance rewarding to the individual? (4) Does performance really matter? (5) Are there obstacles to performing?

      * Has too many assignments unrelated to research so that time is not available to conduct scholarly work.

      * Works in an area in which external funds are not available for scholarly research.

These are but a few of the reasons that may surface in your conversations with a faculty member. It is helpful to understand them if you are to develop a cooperative plan for improving performance.

Identify a plan for improvement.

A plan for improvement should incorporate activities and resources at your command as well as those available from the individual you are helping. Our discussion will be focused on strategies chairpersons can bring to the situation.

Consider two ideas. Use multiple strategies rather than limiting yourself to one. For example, a communications chair in a doctoral-granting institution used the following process with an older assistant professor who had ten years of professional experience before going back for a Ph.D.:

      1. He visited with the individual about areas of interest;

      2. He talked with individuals in the field and called them to discuss the faculty member's research interests;

      3. He encouraged the person to publish from her dissertation;

      4. He contacted individuals in her professional association about the possibility of presenting her research at a national conference;

      5. He worked with the person to discuss how to rewrite conference papers into journal articles, and how to identify appropriate journals in the field for publication.

One sentence summarized the situation for this chair: "We began to get the person into the research process -- thinking about things, doing some research, writing papers, going to national meetings, and taking feedback and turning it into publications."

Next, individualize the improvement plan. Assess whether the plan is consistent with the needs of individuals at their stage of career. The approach needs to differ for senior and junior faculty. Senior faculty require less obtrusive, more subtle and indirect approaches than junior faculty. Practices such as encouraging, supporting, praising, appreciating, and matching interests with resources are more facilitating strategies for senior faculty than junior faculty. For junior faculty, the approach can be more direct, talking with them about the chair's perceptions of their needs and then establishing a plan of activities, including such components as allocating resources, representing the individual, role modeling and mentoring, and supporting and encouraging the person.

1. *Allocating Resources.* Chairs can support faculty, especially junior faculty, by adjusting workloads and assignments, allocating funds, providing information, and finding research equipment. A chairperson in accounting at a research university commented about adjusting workloads:

> I work in the direction of providing released time for research. I've reduced the teaching loads of all faculty so they only teach two classes a quarter and hopefully not more than four preparations during the year. I give faculty released time when they have research projects.

Funds and support services are important in helping untenured faculty members improve their performance. Resources under chairpersons' control often include secretarial assistance, research leaves, travel to professional meetings to present papers, and graduate assistants. An engineering chairperson in a doctoral-granting school described the resources needed by one untenured faculty member:

> An assistant professor right out of school joined the department. The real problem was how to help him get started in the fastest way. I got him involved in our graduate program so that he would have graduate research assistants. I got him some internal support, some equipment money. Finally, I assisted him in getting a foundation award of $60,000 over a three-year period for his own development. All of this gave him a base of support from which to operate and from which to get started.

A tenured faculty member who had "two or three good papers very early in his career went through a fifteen-year dry spell in publishing and didn't write because he had too high standards." His helper, a chair in a social sciences department, provided rewards for publishing:

> I took a "no-nonsense" approach to rewards: I gave him a big salary raise. When he published something, it was extremely good. I saw to it that he received rewards for his research.

Another individual in a music department with a half-time academic appointment and a half-time performing arts position, received from the chairperson information about expectations for tenure:

> I identified what I thought the issues were and set up a series of
> meetings with the dean and with other faculty to talk about the
> criteria for evaluation. After that I visited with the faculty
> member about a five-year schedule of research, performance,
> and teaching, and talked about his schedule to make his research
> time most productive.

These examples illustrate practices of reducing teaching loads, providing "start-up" and equipment moneys, and clarifying expectations for evaluation -- all examples of allocating the resources of assignment, funds, and information.

2. *Representing the individual.* Chairs can assist faculty in improving performance by representing them (or advocating for them) to other individuals. You negotiate with the dean for reduced loads and assignments and forward information to deans about the research progress of individuals. Especially for untenured faculty, chairs network with researchers and scholars both on and off campus to assist the individual. They may put faculty "in touch" with conference planners and funding agencies. A fine arts chair discussed a faculty member who "did not have a research record that would merit tenure." This individual had professional experience outside the academy prior to his doctoral program but he "had difficulty translating experiences into professional research activities." What did the chair do? He visited with him about research interests and then "called individuals on other campuses and put the person in touch with researchers."

Representing individuals on campus provides visibility for their accomplishments. It also leads to important recognition of accomplishments, a strong motivator for an individual to continue producing scholarly works. A finance chair believed in letting others know about the quality of work in the "pipeline":

> People aren't really on top of what is going on -- they only
> evaluate what is published, not the work in the pipeline. My
> problem has been to communicate that the work in progress is
> good and going to be published.

One approach to visibility is to place the individual on important committees so that the person gets to know other faculty. One chairperson commented:

> I've given him good committee assignments that are easy and of
> high visibility so that he can have a good track record for
> promotion. While he waits for his articles to come through, he
> looks good to faculty and administrators.

3. *Role modeling and mentoring.* You can facilitate the research of faculty by collaborating with them on projects and by reviewing and providing feedback on their manuscripts and projects. Chairpersons mentor and share their expertise with untenured faculty by collaborating with them in finding research funds, in selecting general research topics, and in teaming on projects. One chairperson said,

> We worked on collaborative projects. This means involving them in some of my research projects and then making it clear that they need to get their own projects going later on, on their own initiative.

A chairperson was able to encourage an assistant professor in physical education by coupling the faculty member's interests with the assistant professor's coaching interests. Since the scholarly interests of the individual were in the same areas as the chair's, they began collaborating on research. They created a questionnaire, distributed it, analyzed the results, and wrote up the findings. Soon afterward, the faculty member reported the research at a regional conference. Since then, conference coordinators have asked the faculty member to present other research papers. Now she is saying, "This is really great. When can we get ready for next year?"

Collaboration may mean that the chair reacts to faculty grant proposals. An engineering chairperson in a doctoral-granting institution talked about a second-year faculty member who didn't know how to write a grant proposal. In this case, when the individual produced a proposal, the chair provided a thorough review and critique:

> I've spent fifteen to sixteen years in academia watching talented new Ph.D.'s get "ground up" by the system. Some people have the ability to conduct research, but they haven't learned the art of grantsmanship. They lack skills in selling their ideas.

> For one second-year faculty member, I reviewed all his proposals and worked on format and budget. I don't really tell him what kind of research to do because he's not working in my area, but I'm a fairly experienced proposal evaluator. I can read his proposal and tell him whether it's going to hold the interest of the potential funding agency.

Often faculty struggle to understand editors' criticisms and comments on manuscripts. Helping faculty interpret editorial comments on manuscripts is an important form of assistance. A chairperson in a family and human resources department talked about junior faculty being "ravaged" by editorial reviews:

> When junior faculty submit a manuscript to a respectable and
> competitive journal and the manuscript comes back "ravaged"
> by the reviewer, the novice researcher says: "This is the poorest
> manuscript that they have ever received." A negative review,
> however slight, can crush a new faculty member who has put in
> a tremendous amount of time on the paper. The chair needs to
> help the junior faculty member understand that such a review is
> typical, and unless the paper is ruled out completely, to revise,
> revise, and revise.

By reviewing comments from reviewers, by reacting to papers and proposals, and
by working directly with the individual on research projects, the chairperson
supports the continued research improvement of a faculty member.

4. *Supporting and encouraging.* A final set of practices for supporting
faculty involves discovering a faculty member's interests and matching them with
resources, as well as appreciating and acknowledging a faculty member's scholarly
work. For example, a chairperson in special education in a major university
described a tenured faculty member who had no professional publications during
a two-to three-year period. The chairperson explained, "Few attempts had been
made to write grants. Each had resulted in dismal failure." Commenting on this
situation, the chairperson said:

> I first identified the interests of the individual, linked resources
> to his interests, and made myself an integral player, as a good
> colleague or role model, in facilitating his efforts.

Our chairpersons spoke about stressing individual strengths: appreciating
an individual's work and providing encouragement and praise. A psychology
chairperson in a doctoral-granting institution sought to create a better research
atmosphere in his department where "they all had good teaching evaluations, but
none of them had published in years." When the chairperson came to the department,
an associate professor -- one who hadn't published in twelve years -- told him "he
didn't intend to do any research, that he enjoyed teaching, and asked why he should
waste his time on research." In response, the chair "didn't challenge his values" but
showed his support by

> the simple act of acknowledging and letting him know that I
> appreciated the things that he was doing and, when he contributed,
> I made it a point to go to him and say, just casually, "I really
> appreciated the leadership you provided."

Follow-up on the plan.

A final step in improving a faculty member's research performance is to follow up on the plan and strategies to determine whether an individual's productivity improves. Annual conferences or weekly meetings can be used as valuable time to assess progress. In some cases, you may see only a modicum of improvement. One individual said, "We haven't gotten to the point that he's doing any research, but he's talking about it." Another chair commented on the case of a tenured assistant professor in a comprehensive college who lacked a record of scholarly performance. Expectations for this individual were not high:

> I felt it necessary to get him involved in writing, or at least presenting papers where he needed to conduct a literature search to find relevant studies in his field, and then, hopefully, organize some proposals or *a* proposal to develop a research or scholarly study.

When individuals produce, consider promoting or advocating the person's cause by writing positive recommendations for promotion and tenure and visiting with faculty and administrators about the successful performance of the individual.

Suggested Resources

Books

Bowen, H., and Schuster, J.H. *American Professors: A National Resource Imperiled.* New York: Oxford University Press, 1986.

Howard Bowen and Jack Schuster review the current state of academic employment. The study conclusions are drawn from nation-wide interviews with faculty and administrators. Bowen and Schuster discuss several problems facing faculty today, especially in a section titled "The Faculty Fragmented." They include demographic and financial data on faculty across the nation. They discuss academia's deteriorating work environment, its declining social status, and the drain of Ph.D. faculty members to employment beyond the academy. We recommend the description of the increasing research emphasis on many campuses.

Creswell, J.W. *Faculty Research Performance: Lessons from the Sciences and the Social Sciences.* ASHE/ERIC Higher Education Report No. 4. Washington D.C.: Association for the Study of Higher Education, 1985.

John Creswell synthesizes the literature on faculty research performance during the last forty years. He discusses the measures of performance, the correlates of high productivity, and the conceptual explanations of scholarship available in the sociological and social-psychology literature. Overall, Creswell cites networking opportunities; personality; and environmental, sociological, and institutional factors as primary factors influencing research productivity.

Mager, R. F. and Pipe, P. *Analyzing Performance Problems*. Belmont, California: Fearon Pitman Publishers, Inc., 1970.

Robert Mager and Peter Pipe wrote this concise work for managers and trainers attempting to assess and solve problems in worker productivity. The book takes less than an hour to read and is well worth the time spent. The writing is organized in an "if - then" problem analysis flow chart format. Discussion in each chapter follows the progression of the chart
The tendency to solve every problem is discussed and refuted. Skill deficiencies are considered on three levels -- lack of knowledge, lack of practice, and lack of effective feedback. Performance management is discussed as a tool for motivating workers to complete tasks that they don't/ won't do. The final chapter contains a chart and "Quick Reference Checklist" summary which could be used by those without time to read the whole book.

Seldin, P. *Successful Faculty Evaluation Programs*. New York: Coventry Press, 1980.

This work traces several forces contributing to an increased research emphasis on college campuses. Seldin examines faculty evaluation from a number of perspectives. Two chapters, "Institutional Service" and "Research and Publication," may be of special interest.

Seldin, P. *Changing Practices in Faculty Evaluation*. San Francisco: Jossey-Bass, 1984.

Peter Seldin discusses financial conditions within higher education and relates these conditions to faculty members. He reviews the legal system's influences on academic administrative decision-making. Seven experts comment on faculty evaluation related to teaching, research, and service and its impact on higher education. The final chapter of the book is devoted to development of more effective evaluation systems in higher education.

CHAPTER EIGHT

Refocus
Faculty Efforts

Don't let people flounder.
Do a lot of one-on-one relating
[a chairperson in a research university].

Don't give up on anybody [a chairperson in a comprehensive university].

Every faculty member needs a role and needs support.
We'll help a person in mid-career who needs reorientation
or who wants to change direction -- if it's appropriate for
the program and the university and we can find some
resources [a chairperson in a research university].

Some faculty members find new challenges and maintain enthusiasm throughout their careers. With gentle prodding and suggestions, others find renewed vigor. Some find it through expanding or modifying their areas of interest, others through sabbaticals or leaves of absence. Some faculty, however, need help initiating a major refocus in order to remain productive and excited about their careers.

Refocusing may become necessary due to lack of motivation, family difficulties, personality traits, aging issues, or because of shifts in the priority or mission of an academic department. Faculty may have little control over a changing work environment that renders their skills or areas of expertise obsolete for department needs.

"Excellent" chairpersons spoke about *their* responsibility for assisting faculty refocus efforts, and clearly indicated that chairs should be a force in helping faculty move ahead with their professional lives. They also emphasized that helping faculty is not simply a technical series of events which can be laid out and forgotten but a process of negotiating and renegotiating efforts and rewards.

This chapter explores the process chairpersons might use to help faculty refocus their efforts. This process consists of four steps:

1. Detect the signs of a problem through information gathering.

2. Once a problem is evident, explore options with the individual by assessing feelings, needs, and interests.

3. Mutually design a plan for intervention that includes coming to an agreement on goals and proposed direction.

4. Arrange for activities, resources and feedback to implement the plan.

Detecting the signs.

The forces leading to change are complex and often difficult to identify. However, an astute chair may observe early signs that faculty are not experiencing continued vigor. If faculty do not adjust, their behavior may become chronic, leading to disengagement and even burnout. Thus, it is important for chairpersons to gather information about potential problems through personal observations, annual evaluation conferences, and from visiting with students and colleagues. Chairs might look for signs that include:

1. *Dissatisfaction* with work roles or assignments:

Many faculty were hired who were specialists, and it seemed that every time somebody was hired, it took away from something he was doing. It reached a point where he obviously was just given whatever was left or needed to be picked up. There was very little professional opportunity left for this individual [a chairperson in a research university].

2. *Lack or loss of enthusiasm,* getting stale, or suffering burnout:

She started to come to class late and withdrew into herself [a chairperson in a liberal arts college].

3. *Performing minimal duties,* doing only what crosses their desks.

This person taught classes and that's about all he did [a chairperson in a comprehensive university].

4. *Negative attitude:*

He was perceived by others as not having a positive attitude. He responded negatively and defensively [a chairperson in a research university].

Rosabeth Moss Kanter (1981, pp. 36-37) described individuals who are "movers" and those who are "stuck" in their jobs. Characteristics of both types of individuals, shown in Table 1, might be useful for department chairs who are looking for signs of a problem.

Table 1

*Characteristics of Movers and Stuck Faculty. ***

Characteristic	Movers	Stuck
Aspirations	High goals	Low goals, loss of enthusiasm
Self-esteem	Self-confident; willing to take risks	Low self-esteem; cautious/conservative; looks for formulas
Connection to work	A workaholic	Becomes disengaged; "retires on the job;" spends time off campus or on outside pursuits (e.g., professional associations)
Relationships	Keeps political alliances alive; concerned about larger issues in the organization	Falls back on protective peer groups and seeks outside sources for esteem
How dissatisfaction is handled	Active, constructive forms of protest; feels decisionmakers will listen	Petty griper; subtle saboteur; blocks committee work; resists innovation; makes life difficult for others

*Source: Kanter, 1981, pp. 36-37

Explore options with the individual.

If any of these signs are present, consider exploring options with the individual by assessing feelings, interests, and needs. This step involves the crucial practices of *listening, understanding,* and *comforting.* Todd Furniss, an advocate of faculty career changes, speaks of motivational issues:

> The motivational questions are tough ones for the established academic. They are probably toughest at the stage when the faculty member has not yet acknowledged the strength of the push to change what he is doing and has discussed it with no one. A common element to all the techniques of intervention in career counseling and personal therapy is providing the environment in which the client will begin to talk about his situation with a view to improving it and not just complaining about it (1981, p. 100).

Regarding a senior faculty member who faced changing institutional expectations for scholarly work, a chairperson in a doctoral-granting school said:

> He had my full support. I was empathetic and understanding about his inactivity in research performance because it was not being reinforced. I let him know I did not expect immediate turnaround and that over a period of years we expected to see him get back into the mainstream.

Unfortunately, some faculty get stuck in routines or ruts and cannot break the inertia by themselves. Unless someone -- sometimes a colleague but more often the chairperson -- initiates an active exploration process, a faculty member may begin a downward spiral, difficult to reverse. He or she becomes isolated and disenchanted. When this happens, all parties lose -- faculty member, chairperson, student, department, and institution. If this situation can be changed, all can gain.

A senior faculty member in one case wanted to do something new. The comments of a chairperson in a comprehensive college provided a sense of creative exploration.

> Several years ago a faculty member in his late fifties was getting stale. He wanted to have a new opportunity. He liked to travel and went abroad every summer. The department has numerous foreign students in whom the professor had always shown interest. Their language skills in English were often poor. Perhaps he would like to gain the skills to teach them English as a second language? I noted a further benefit. When he retired,

he would have a skill that would let him get a job in all sorts of fascinating places. He is now getting a master's in teaching English as a second language.

In the process of exploration, the chair helped the faculty member blend individual strengths and interests with departmental needs. While carving out a teaching area which the department wanted, the individual was also setting himself up with skills useful for retirement or a second career.

Successful exploration of options requires considerable reality testing. A chairperson of a comprehensive university commented:

> I'm getting them to think through the options. I say, "This is the direction the department is going, and it will be hard for you to get back into the mainstream. We can try for that, or we can try to get you into something else in the university."

If there is a level of trust and support, one can mention almost any option and the discussion will be seen as helpful -- even if the option represents a major change, such as working in a different campus unit or seeking employment at another institution. To develop this point further, the same chairperson reported that his department had a number of non-researchers who "moved on." "But," he emphasized, "that doesn't mean they were booted out." For example, he had one member, a clinician, who is now working at the campus clinical center where "he is happy."

Finding the unique match of interests and needs is further clarified by a chair of a major land-grant university:

> People are different. If you try to blend them into a mold, they'll resist because they are not comfortable with it. But if you work with them to find their strengths and interests (all the people we're working with are intelligent), most of them can make contributions.

Helping a faculty member clarify feelings about his or her personal situation calls for one-on-one conversations between the chair and the individual and the skillful development of active listening skills. A research university chair in business described a long-time department member who had experienced burnout.

> He taught classes and that was about all; he was perceived by others as not having a positive attitude, but it was just the way in which he expressed himself. We have now made significant progress in turning the situation around.

It took a lot of time and one-on-one conversations. We did not talk about the personality traits and problems I just described. Rather, I found positive ways in which I could give this person some additional responsibility, some opportunities to excel in areas where I felt he could excel, and a few small jobs in which he would be successful and motivate him to do more. It was not a matter of sitting down and saying, "You have problems." In fact, we didn't even identify them.

The chair went on to say that in the last two years he has seen a significant turnaround in the way this person reacts to situations.

His manner is much more favorable rather than negative and defensive as before. The person has become deeply involved in the use of microcomputers. In fact, it's commonly accepted that this individual is probably one of the most proficient in the use of the microcomputer in accounting classes. He assists other faculty members, whereas earlier he had done none of this kind of activity. It's a significant turnaround in interest and a willingness to help other people.

In refocusing situations, when chairs and faculty explore feelings and professional and personal satisfactions it leads to defining options or alternatives that may fit the interest of the faculty member. The discovery process often moves slowly, requiring numerous conversations and substantial time commitment. In some of the classical literature and in adult development research, this time of moving from the old (known) to the new (unknown) requires some "wandering through the wilderness" or experiencing what William Bridges in *Transitions* (1980) describes as the "neutral zone." At this critical stage in a person's career, the availability of chairpersons and colleagues who listen can lessen the anguish and ease the transition.

Mutually design a plan for intervention.

Once the faculty member commits to retrain in a new area or refocus efforts, the chairperson can help the individual develop and structure a plan.

A term from the social-psychology field, "psychological contract," captures the essence of this step. The term is used by Edgar Schein from MIT's Sloan School of Management.

Through various kinds of symbolic and actual events, a "psychological contract" is formed which defines what the employee will give in the way of effort and contribution in exchange for challenging or rewarding work, acceptable working conditions, organizational rewards in the form of pay and benefits, and an organizational future in the form of a promise of promotion or other forms of career advancement. This contract is "psychological" in that the actual terms remain implicit; they are not written down anywhere. But the mutual expectations formed between the employee and the employer function like a contract in that if either party fails to meet the expectations, serious consequences will follow -- demotivation, turnover, lack of advancement or termination (Schein, 1978, p. 132).

Although faculty are loath to consider themselves "employees" and chairpersons are not traditionally viewed as "employers," the "contract" model is useful because it emphasizes the implicit or unwritten rules that may operate between chairpersons and their faculty.

In view of changes during a faculty member's career, one element of this "contract" is continual negotiation between chairs and their faculty.

The psychological contract changes in important ways as the person goes through a career and life cycle, because his or her needs change in important ways. Similarly, what the organization expects of the individual changes with changes in job or role. Thus, one might expect that in the mid- and late-career there is a growing likelihood that new disappointments will arise because the individual effort and the organization's rewards may be based upon assumptions which were more appropriate to an earlier career or life stage. Rather than re-motivating the person, a better solution might be to renegotiate the psychological contract and to adjust expectations on both sides to new realities (Schein, 1978, p. 122).

In addition to the psychological commitment of the two parties, the "contract" may translate into acquisition of resources, reduction of bureaucratic obstacles, and reassignment of duties.

Arrange for activities, resources, and feedback.

Once an agreement has been reached with the faculty member on goals and proposed direction, the chairperson should complete the four-step refocusing process:

1. Identify a sequence of activities, such as schedule changes, reducing or reassigning teaching loads, and suggesting a timeframe to meet the goals;

2. Commit resources and support for the activities, such as student or clerical help, travel to meetings and internship sites, educational materials, tuition payments, and professional leaves;

3. Structure open feedback and evaluate to monitor and ensure necessary alterations in the plan.

Illustration of the process.

A chair of communication arts in a small comprehensive, private university used the four-step process to meet the long-term developmental needs of the department and a faculty member. The chairperson described the background and sequence of preparing a faculty member to teach in the public relations area in the department.

Detect the signs. The public relations sequence here is a relatively new sequence. Before we started it, we had students visit with us about such a sequence, but there was really no place in the university where they could get the training. Compounding the problem was the fact that we didn't have anybody trained in public relations in the department.

Explore options. There was one person, though, with a background in organizational communication who had done some consulting in public relations. I approached this individual and he expressed an interest in teaching an introductory course in public relations.

Mutually design a plan. With that in mind, we did some quick homework about what could be included in an introductory course. We looked at textbooks and articles about speech communication and public relations. We figured we could probably do it without much trouble.

Arrange for activities, resources, and feedback. This gentleman was going to enhance his education. We worked together to develop an application for a Regency Award. We were fortunate, we received the support of the dean. I think we got that because we could show it was going to ultimately increase our credit hours which, as you know, everybody always likes to hear.

The Board of Regents gave this faculty member the award. He spent three months in the summer visiting different public relations agencies in the area. Over the next couple years we supported the faculty member in the public relations area. For example, I paid his dues to the Public Relations Association out of the department's budget. We also arranged scheduling so that he could attend the local chapter of the Public Relations Society. We invited outside people to speak to students on a variety of topics. We supported travel to conventions.

A chair's role is to creatively help faculty move in new directions and to identify resources for these moves. Without such efforts, unsatisfactory situations are often ignored and no adjustments are made to develop the kind of relationship necessary for continued productivity. The examples above show the chairperson's ability to assess talent and to be able to negotiate the "psychological contract," an integration of departmental and individual needs.

Some institutions provide formal programs to help faculty develop refocusing "plans." One example of this is the NUPROF Faculty Renewal and Redirection Program at the University of Nebraska-Lincoln. Faculty in this program are allowed time and structured opportunities for career assessment. They study personal growth and develop an "action plan" with goals, activities, and timeframes for renewal and redirection. This "plan" evolves from answering six sets of questions:

1. Situational Statement:

    a. Where are we now?

    b. What needs to be modified or changed?

2. Goals and Objectives:

    a. What goals are you trying to achieve

    b. How will this benefit you?

    c. How will this benefit the institution?

3. Activities and Timetable to Realize the Goals and Objectives:

    a. What are the first steps?

    b. What is the sequence of activities and expected timeframe? (A flowchart or similar method may be helpful.)

4. Support Needed to Realize the Plan:

   a. What resource people are needed to accomplish the objectives?

   b. What will they do?

   c. What financial resources are needed? Where will you get them?

   d. What support (including allocated time) do you need from administrators?

5. Evaluation of the Plan:

   a. How will you know when you achieve the objectives?

   b. Who else can help you measure your accomplishments?

   c. How will you monitor your progress enroute?

6. Future Directions After the Plan:

   a. What future steps will be important?

Although the questions may be different in other growth programs, common elements of the NUPROF and other similar projects are the opportunities for career assessment, development of peer and administrative support, and the identification of new growth experiences.

Suggested Resources

Books

Bridges, W. *Transitions: Making Sense of Life's Changes.* Reading, MA: Addison-Wesley, 1980.

William Bridges's writings describe the personal process involved in moving from one life situation or position to another. He describes a "neutral zone" between endings and beginnings. Someone in a "neutral zone" needs a "guide" to progress through the transition. Words or actions may be less important or helpful than the fact that someone is "available."

Clark, S., and Lewis, D. *Faculty Vitality and Institutional Productivity.*
New York: Teachers College, 1985.

Shirley Clark and Darrell Lewis are among those who pioneered the concept of faculty vitality — a powerful yet ambiguous concept. These authors have compiled an impressive selection of writings from well-known authors to describe the important relationship of organizational context to faculty vigor and productivity.

Furniss, W. T. *Reshaping Faculty Careers.* Washington D.C.: American
Council on Education, 1981.

Todd Furniss was one of the first authors to explicitly address creative options in faculty career development. He provides a range of possibilities within and outside the academic institution for middle- and late-career academics to satisfy career needs. Furniss challenges sacred assumptions about academic careers and provides a structure to help faculty address career related crises. Specific problems in academic employment are discussed including career changes, career enhancement, and development of new faculty members. An appendix contains discussion of retirement issues.

Nelson, W. *Renewal of the Teacher Scholar.* Washington, D.C.: Association
of American Colleges, 1981.

William Nelson's writing focuses on the small liberal arts colleges. Nelson discusses the ways that small colleges have met the challenge of maintaining faculty vigor. He masterfully cites examples to demonstrate that, even with limited resources, much can be accomplished to keep faculty members active.

Schein, E. *Career Dynamics: Matching Individual and Organizational
Needs.* Reading, MA: Addison-Wesley, 1978.

Edgar Schein of the Sloan School of Management at MIT provides a useful and pioneering work on examining careers in organizations. Schein demonstrates that the satisfaction of both individual and organizational needs can be orchestrated by insightful leaders and managers. He highlights mid-career issues that particularly affect the "psychological contract." See additional notes on this book in the "Suggested Resources" section of the next chapter.

CHAPTER NINE

Address Personal Issues of Faculty

Chairpersons need to carefully assess their personal reaction to the pain level of confronting personal problems and initiate institutional procedures to help faculty members [a philosophy chairperson at a major research university].

It [addressing personal problems] was where I felt most out of my element [a modern language chairperson at a research university].

The personal issues and problems of individual faculty members are a potential threat to the professional productivity of academic departments. If individual problems are not addressed, others in the department will have to pick up the responsibility. Though chairs may feel "out of their element" and experience the "pain" of a frustrating and difficult situation, they are often called upon by faculty and administrators to address the personal issues of faculty.

These situations can be roughly categorized into at least five areas:

1. Relationship problems with students, staff, and faculty;

2. Difficulty associated with dual careers;

3. Exclusion and alienation in the department;

4. Health problems;

5. Personal disorganization.

In response to these issues, how can chairpersons assist? Reflect on the following questions as you read this chapter:

1. Is the personal issue of the faculty member short-term or long-term (chronic)?

2. What are the signs of an individual with a short-term problem?

3. What strategies would a chair use with a short-term problem?

4. What are the signs of an individual with chronic personal problems?

5. What strategies would a chair use with a long-term (chronic) problem?

Short-term versus long-term issues.

Short-term issues are those of short duration which diminish in importance or disappear quickly. Personal "crises" such as individual loss, change in family or financial status, and medical issues, can create situations in which faculty members temporarily demonstrate a lack of concentration, emotional upset, and disorientation. From the adult development literature, we know these "crises" and demands are predictable life experiences and that, with emotional support and some direct help, individuals usually work their way through them and make adjustments. People are just trying to achieve balance in their lives.

Chairs might look for the following signs of problems:

1. *Severe loss or separation:* death of a significant other or divorce.

2. *Changes in family status:* children leaving; children coming back home; aging parents; elderly parents moving into the house; single-parent status.

3. *Changes in work status:* having a new job or role; adjusting to a mate having a job outside the home or a new job.

4. *Added financial responsibility:* buying a house; sending children to college.

5. *Personal aging issues:* physical changes; passing age benchmarks (40, 50, 60); loss of energy.

6. *Health problems:* anxiety about health; short-term surgery; short-term depression.

We recommend several strategies for addressing temporary personal problems:

1. *Become aware of the concern* through "heart-to-heart" talks and listening to the individual.

2. *Protect the individual* during the troubled time by being a "buffer" for a short period, reducing demands or workload, and adjusting responsibilities so the individual can take time off to address needs.

3. *Seek outside help* by referring the individual to counselors for short-term psychological help or by enlisting the help of senior faculty who know the individual.

Sometimes personal problems persist and become chronic. Working with long-term problems can be frustrating. These problems include alcoholism, psychiatric disorders, habitual interpersonal difficulties, inability to cope with departmental and academic expectations, and individual personality traits such as difficult and uncooperative behaviors, aggressive behaviors, "weird behaviors" (for example, "blurting out," "off-color comments"), and severe withdrawal.

The following brief scenarios illustrate situations chairpersons may encounter:

A philosophy chair in a major research university discussed the case of a fifty-year-old full professor who frequently cancelled classes and reported being sick. The graduate students began to draw away from him. The quality and quantity of his work was on a downhill slide. Junior faculty were covering more and more of his responsibilities, yet he was in the regular salary range with everyone else as if nothing was happening. This caused a morale problem within the department.

A chairperson of a music department in a comprehensive university described a faculty member who was past sixty-five but wouldn't have to retire until he was seventy. He had serious health problems which left him with little energy, although he was a well-respected faculty member.

A chairperson of plant sciences in a land-grant university described a faculty member who had been difficult and uncooperative. "I found a negative attitude toward him by faculty in the department, especially senior faculty."

A chairperson of a criminal justice department in a comprehensive university spoke of "an outspoken, critical, impetuous, short-fused faculty member. My first day on the job I went to her lab where she proceeded to rant and rave for thirty minutes about her disappointment with professional opportunities, with her colleagues, and with the progress of the department."

A chairperson of music in a comprehensive university commented about an outstanding academic who by the third year was "completely bogged down" in coursework and "became very paranoid. He thought the students were doing things to him, didn't sleep for weeks on end, and blurted out bizarre things. It was obvious he needed psychiatric help."

A chairperson of English in a comprehensive university described a faculty member with severe personal family problems. "It involves his wife, who has mental problems. It's just a very difficult situation in terms of her willingness to be helped. She thinks that everybody else has the problem. She's been hospitalized and institutionalized a couple times."

These long-term issues require more elaborate interventions than the short-term issues.

A process for intervening in chronic cases.

A chairperson in criminal justice at a comprehensive college talked about a general process model he would use with faculty experiencing chronic problems. Four steps were involved: (1) developing an awareness of the issue; (2) holding a "colleague-to-colleague" discussion about the issue; (3) using authority of the chair position; and, if necessary, (4) initiating formal procedures to modify faculty behavior.

Become aware of the issue or concern. As with all professional-personal development issues and concerns, chairpersons need to be aware of signs and symptoms. These include gathering information through personal observations (for example, looking for withdrawal, aggressiveness, and mental difficulties) and obtaining feedback from students and colleagues. Without this fundamental awareness, the helping process will be ungrounded. In this step, the practices of observing, listening, and probing are particularly crucial.

Hold a colleague-to-colleague discussion. "Chairpersons initiate the first level of response as a colleague and friend," one of the chairs said. The message given is, "I have a concern and how can I help you?" There is encouragement to get whatever help is needed to address the issue. This colleague-to-colleague attention was summarized by an associate of one chair who said, "He talks to people for a living." Other chairpersons in our study also reinforced the colleague-to-colleague discussion approach.

A chairperson of a drama department in a liberal arts college suggested initiating these conversations. "It's something I do because I cherish my colleagues. It's something I would be doing whether I was a chairperson or not."

This "colleague-to-colleague" involvement is emphasized by a chairperson of history in a comprehensive university. "I get involved in their lives—not merely academics but financial matters and problems with children."

Chairpersons realize it's not always easy to have these conversations, but they sometimes garner results because the faculty member realizes there is a problem and that modifications at this stage may avoid more formal and adversative procedures later. Establishing an open atmosphere and giving feedback are particularly useful, such as in the following practices:

> Allow him to ventilate.

> Listen to the reason that deadlines are missed, and let her express her ideas.

> Do not minimize the problem. Confront him with the problem.

> Stress the importance of meeting deadlines and how it affects others.

> Create a professional crisis equal to the personal crisis.

Use authority of your position. If you are unsuccessful in modifying behavior or persuading a colleague to seek help, use a more direct intervention to address the issue. Options include: *providing new areas of responsibility for the individual;*

> I removed him from an assignment he felt inadequate about and reassigned him to other duties.

having the individual see how others addressed problems;

> I had faculty eat breakfast together once a month away from the university," or "I got him involved in workshops to give him insight into other people's problems.

and referring the individual to counselors or self-help groups.

> I encouraged him to go into counseling, or I assisted in getting him psychiatric help.

The chairs noted that this phase required patience, skill, and innovation and provided clear messages to the individual: "I'm here to see you get the help"; "I'll take you out of class or whatever is necessary, but continuing the same pattern is unacceptable." Faculty members in this circumstance have crossed over the line of being responsible for their own behavior, and the chair must intervene.

Quite often chair intervention leads to outside referrals for counseling or psychiatric help. The use of an outside referral system is illustrated by a chairperson of a natural sciences department at a land-grant research university who described a highly emotional faculty member:

> The faculty member is a hard-driving person who doesn't let up. These pressures mounted and resulted in a couple of emotional blowups with yelling and door slamming in the office of an administrator. A personal friend who knows his family suggested a history of manic-depressive behavior. I've pointed out to him examples of my behavior to prove I considered him trustworthy and to prove I dealt honestly and openly with him. I've had a number of very patient discussions with him. I made an extra effort to follow through on any commitments to him. Some of the administration thinks he's still a bomb waiting to go off. We have managed to get him psychological counseling. He may need psychiatric help.

As this example demonstrates, chairpersons are forced to make "mental health assessments," however tentative, and to aid individuals in entering the mental health system for treatment.

A chairperson of philosophy from a major research university took the approach of referring the individual for outside help and lessening workload demands:

> This was an individual who came to us as a Ph.D. candidate. He was finishing his degree at a Big Ten School, had strong professional experience and very good academic credentials. We had expected a great deal out of him. As things turned out, he got bogged down in coursework, and I'm not sure of all the pressures. The next thing we knew he was acting very funny — talking of not being able to sleep for weeks on end and just blurting things out.
>
> It was very stressful for all of us. I set about getting him psychiatric help. I talked to him, tried to understand his problems and worked through the [university] machinery so the man was able to get the help he needed with the full support of the school. I was able to wind my way through the bureaucracy and sort of grease the way so that things happened.

> After a time, I gave him a semester off. Then I brought him back in the summer to let him try one course. That didn't work out satisfactorily, so I sent him home to rest again until fall. We gave him a course in the fall and he wasn't able to handle that. Finally, we just arranged for him to have full pay for the rest of the year and to make sure he was still on full-time status so he was able to get the kind of psychiatric help he needed.

Eventually, the faculty member left, but the chair believed that the strategies were successful in that he provided a "bridge" or "link" for the individual to leave af.er seeking a number of opportunities for him to step back into the academic setting. "Sometimes success is helping someone accept that the situation isn't going to work," concluded the chairperson.

A recent trend on some college and university campuses is to have faculty assistance programs for individuals with personal problems. You may be familiar with Employee or Faculty Assistance Programs (often referred to as EAP's or FAP's) which help faculty and staff confront problems — both on and off the job — that can seriously affect their productivity. Such programs provide initial counseling and referral for commonly occurring personal issues: marital/family problems, drug and alcohol abuse, personal finance issues, and emotional stress. Most programs provide individual consultation to administrators on how to handle personal problems. Key questions chairpersons might ask themselves about the personal assistance network on their campus include:

> 1. What resources are available to help a person with a chronic problem? Is there an off-campus EAP? Often the best sources of this information are other chairs, the personnel department or the psychology department.
>
> 2. If there is an EAP, who is eligible? What services are offered? How are the services used? Who is the contact person?
>
> 3. If there is not an EAP available, what other referrals are possible? Is there a medical center or campus clinic which will address personal issues?
>
> 4. If institutionally sponsored services are not available, who would be available and what is the procedure for using the services?

Chairpersons need to personally know a resource they can contact for referrals or have someone they can call who will identify a creditable, effective mental health professional. These individuals may be a contact on or off campus.

You need to have the sequence of procedures and actual people in mind *before* situations arise. Pre-planning will help to prevent impulse or panic decisions.

As a last resort, initiate formal procedures. In some of the more inimical cases, formal procedures are needed to bring about changed behavior. These include:

1. Formal written notification of the concerns and reasons for the initiated procedure -- freezing salary or commencing some personnel action.

2. A formal meeting with the individual to discuss the contents of the letter -- "they need to know the rules and expectations."

3. Follow-through on the procedures initiated.

No doubt chairpersons prefer that issues can be resolved with early action steps. When more formalized personnel procedures are employed, issues can become polarized with "gut-wrenching" consequences for all involved. For example, faculty in the department may choose sides or rush to the defense of the "persecuted" faculty member. In one case, the chairperson responded to faculty concerns about an individual by "achieving a departmental agreement on how to address the faculty member in crisis so that there would be no move to scapegoat him." Not surprisingly, chairpersons also monitor procedures and strategies to avoid violating due process or triggering possible grievances or lawsuits. In this fourth step, chairpersons need to demonstrate firmness as well as compassion. A good description of the ideal is characterized by Fisher and Ury as "be soft on the people, hard on the problem" (Fisher and Ury, 1981, p. 13).

Certainly, chair's fears and anxieties sometimes inhibit formal actions. A social sciences chairperson at a comprehensive university captures the dilemma:

There is more freedom and flexibility at the chair level, yet it is generally perceived just the opposite. Rather than back into the formalized procedures, I notify faculty when formal procedures are begun and, in many cases, suggest they may want to retain the services of an attorney (especially in sexual harassment or any suspected criminal cases).

As a standard operating procedure, chairpersons need to keep upper-level higher administrators informed about what is happening. On a more personal level, chairpersons might determine how they will respond when and if their own popularity, respect and fairness come into question because of the pressure they put on faculty to make adjustments.

Consider whether there would be risk in *not* initiating procedures. Will the problem be passed on to the next chair? Will faculty hide behind the concept of academic freedom that says, "I can do whatever I want—I'm not accountable"? If the choice is made not to address chronic personal problems, chairpersons should recognize they are possibly compounding the situation for the individual faculty and for the department in the long run. Often individuals follow a downward spiral they cannot seem to reverse without help, creating morale problems for the department. Chairperson intervention can be uncomfortable in the short run. Confrontations can generate denial and acrimonious feelings, and the outcomes are uncertain. In the long run, the intervention may create a break in destructive patterns and provide opportunities for new decisions by faculty.

Suggested Resources

Books and Periodicals

Boice, R. "Counseling Colleagues." *The Personnel and Guidance Journal,* 1982, *61*, 239-240.

Robert Boice, a psychologist-faculty development specialist, has written about counseling colleagues and identification of personal issues. Boice sees difficulty in addressing personal issues because professionals feel "self-reliant" and are reluctant to seek help. He suggests that as professional pressures and changes multiply, more attention to personal concerns will be needed. Boice initially helped faculty with mental blocks in writing and soon was involved in helping faculty deal with personal issues.

Schein, E. *Career Dynamics: Matching Individual and Organizational Needs.* Reading, Maine: Addison-Wesley, 1978.

This book is also discussed in the previous chapter. Part I, "The Individual and the Life Cycle," provides insights and a conceptual framework for looking at personal development. Schein integrates ideas of numerous developmental theorists into a framework of useful observations about personal and family demands and expectations. He also suggests constructive coping strategies useful for department chairpersons.

Scanlon, W.F. *Alcoholism and Drug Abuse in the Workplace: Employee Assistance Programs.* New York, NY: Praeger Publishers, 1986.

Scanlon's book contains a review of employee assistance programs. It covers the history, philosophy, and functions of EAP's. The impact of alcohol and drug abuse on the U.S.A. is considered from historical, economic, corporate and rehabilitation perspectives.

TIAA-CREF Research Dialogue. "Employee Assistance Programs in Educational Institutions." No. 16, February, 1988.

This dialogue allows chairpersons to view the nature and use of Employee Assistance Programs (EAP's). For a detailed account of the development and scope of EAP's in higher education also see: Thoreson, R.W., and Hosakawa, E.P. *Employee Assistance Programs in Higher Education.* Springfield, Illinois: Charles C. Thomas, 1984.

CHAPTER TEN

Build an Agenda

*I enjoy seeing the progress of faculty in their careers,
building up the department, and being told I'm appreciated.
[an agricultural chair in a research university]*

*It's important to recognize that chairs have power --
maybe more perceived than real. They can do almost
anything if they are supported by the faculty. [a
communications chair in a comprehensive college]*

Our discussion has focused on building a positive work environment for faculty. It began with your own self-development as a chair. It continued in a departmental context with your role as an "academic leader." Finally, the building of a positive work environment for faculty hinged on your ability to establish sound rapport through good interpersonal relations. These strategies, as we call them, were applied to faculty undergoing predictable growth phases in their careers. These phases related to faculty needs: for orientation and adjustment to new departments; development as effective teachers and scholars; refocusing efforts at mid-career to better contribute to departments; and solving personal issues that detract from overall individual and departmental performance. Phases such as these provide fertile opportunity for chairpersons to apply the strategies introduced in this book.

In this chapter, we synthesize the strategies into an overall framework for building a positive work environment for faculty. This framework has four key dimensions: develop *people*, consider the institutional *context*, acknowledge the *process*, and make a difference in *outcomes*.

Four dimensions of the building process.

1. Be sensitive to the developmental growth of people and the organization.

A developmental perspective is based on the premise that individuals grow and develop professionally in response to changes in their personal lives and in their work environment. We recommend that this perspective become an integral focus in your department. It may appear as an agenda item for your next departmental meeting. It can be discussed when faculty assignments are made. A growth perspective can pervade all aspects of departmental work.

Think in terms of the career phases of faculty. The needs of beginning staff differ from those of more senior, experienced staff. Faculty begin a career experiencing personal needs of adjusting, belonging, identifying, and learning about the new work environment. They may find success as teachers or scholars, or they may encounter setbacks. They struggle with student evaluations; they lecture over the heads of students; they become devastated by negative feedback about their teaching; they revel in the joys of teaching. In the research area, they may struggle with negative comments of reviewers, lack a focused line of research or continuity in their scholarship, misplace their priorities jeopardizing their chances for tenure or promotion, or publish a seminal work.

By mid- and late-career, the survival question is no longer germane as they become promoted and tenured. But new difficulties and opportunities arise as their level of performance varies. New interests develop. Faculty accomplish one benchmark and consider the next. They renegotiate the "psychological contract" with chairs. Classroom syllabi may no longer be relevant; few research studies may be undertaken because of increased interests in campus committee work or teaching. They experience personal issues such as health problems that interfere with their departmental performance.

To better understand faculty experiences at different stages of an academic career, a chair might turn to Baldwin and Blackburn's (1981) table that outlines five stages of an academic career (i.e., assistant professors in the first three years of teaching, assistant professor with more than three years of teaching, associate professors, and full professors more than five years from retirement, full professors within five years of retirement), in addition to faculty experiences such as career ambitions, enthusiasm, adjustments, disappointments, and familiarity with the organization.

Chairs experience professional change and growth, too. They go through phases in their careers including entry-level socialization and learning about the position, establishing rapport with faculty and other unit administrators, attempting to reach long-range goals for the department and its people, and a phasing-out period which includes a resocialization to the faculty role or accepting more senior administrative posts. These phases, not well detailed in the scholarly literature about chairing a department, are predictable and represent times for chairs to reflect on their own progress and goals. Schein's (1978) stages in the career cycle offer insight into the general issues and specific tasks to be confronted. Schein's stages parallel the experiences of chairs, such as entry into the world of work, basic training, full membership in early- and mid-career, mid-career crisis, late-career nonleadership and leadership, and decline and disengagement leading to retirement.

The department, too, is undergoing organizational growth. Organizational theorists talk about three stages in organizational development: creation and early development, transformations, and decline and termination (Kimberly, Miles, and Associate, 1981). Undoubtedly, academic departments as formal organizations are experiencing predictable growth phases. This suggests that individuals in departments acknowledge changes that are occurring, actively discuss them, and recognize that units do not remain static and unchanging. Chairs might ask themselves the following questions:

1. Do I tailor my strategies so that the needs of faculty at different stages of their career are met?

2. How am I growing and developing professionally?

3. How is our department changing and developing?

2. Understand the departmental, institutional, and disciplinary context in which this growth occurs.

Individual and departmental growth does not occur in a vacuum. Consider how the setting affects growth. Individuals respond to this setting differently, thus chairs need to continually assess the strengths, interests, and needs of faculty. But do not stop here: match the individual needs to departmental priorities, the institutional vision, and when important, to discipline needs.

As a case in point, this book advances five specific faculty situations often faced by chairpersons. This list is not meant to be exhaustive; faculty issues and situations are bounded by the context in which they arise. For example, in institutions with different missions and goals, the faculty issues will vary. Bowen and Schuster (1986) discuss the different personal educational and world outlooks of individuals from different disciplines and the differentiated institutional groups based on college values and goals. In our study, college teaching issues surfaced more in our analysis of liberal arts schools and comprehensive colleges. Scholarly research questions arose from our interviews with chairs in research universities. The strategies chairs use may be discipline or field specific. Scientists in the hard or physical sciences are more concerned about funds for establishing laboratories and equipment purchases. Psychology chairs spoke more frequently than other chairs about the interpersonal processes involved in helping faculty. In short, the context is important in which chairs assess and hopefully meet the needs of faculty.

View the strategies in this book as working best in one-on-one interactions with faculty or as interactions with *all* faculty in the department. "Excellent" chairs discussed both situations. Among the possibilities for one-on-one opportunities are:

1. Informal day-to-day interactions;

2. Annual performance reviews at the end of the year;

3. Helping faculty establish goals for the year;

4. Social gatherings.

In addition, chairs can impact the entire department through:

1. Sharing their vision for the department at a departmental meeting;

2. Creating an atmosphere where the vision is actively explored through discussion, displays, and setting an example;

3. Sharing information through the stimulus of an outside speaker or a departmental roundtable discussion;

4. Discussing what constitutes good teaching, research, or service in the department;

5. Talking about their approaches to "advocacy" for the entire department (using realistic, specific language).

Undoubtedly, the repertoire of involvement depends on time, individual style, and the willingness of faculty and the entire department. Chairs in a positive department look for approaches to broaden their involvement and recognize individual and departmental opportunities to make an impact. Chairs might ask themselves:

1. In what ways do I assess the individual needs of my faculty?

2. What important department, institution, or disciplinary priorities must I link these needs to?

3. When do I interact with faculty individually? Do these opportunities make an impact?

4. When do I interact with the entire faculty? Do these opportunities make an impact?

3. Acknowledge that building is a process.

This orientation means that faculty change is a growth process involving identifiable stages in which chairs can intervene or assist. A chair can enter these stages in any order. Assistance is recognized as an on-going process, often involving several months or even years.

As we reviewed the processes used by "excellent" chairs, we found a four-step model that typified the approaches used:

1. Detect the signs of faculty needs;

2. Explore the options individually with the person;

3. Collaboratively develop a plan for action;

4. Enact the plan and monitor its results.

This model reinforces a "systems" approach often found in the change literature. For example, Kirkpatrick (1985) advances a slightly more elaborate seven-step model managers might use to bring about change in workers: determine the need or desire for a change, prepare a tentative plan, analyze probable reactions, make a final decision, establish a timetable, communicate the change, and implement the change.

Regardless of the model you use, we all recognize that changing someone else's behavior is difficult. We need to enter the process fully aware that individuals do not change until they are ready to do so. We cannot expect a 100% success rate. Chairs should look for small signs of success, incremental changes. A chair should consider whether the individual whom you want to assist will accept your help. Maybe someone else is more appropriate (e.g., a fellow faculty member, a chaplain, an Employee Assistance counselor, a consultant from the Faculty Development Center). Finally, recognize that the process of helping faculty will take your time, energy, and commitment. As the chorus chimes in Act II of Gilbert and Sullivan's *The Pirates of Penzance,* "a policeman's lot is not a happy one." Chairs might ask themselves,

1. What steps do I go through helping a faculty member change?

2. Are my expectations for change realistic?

4. Recognize that chairs can make a difference.

Several outcomes may result from chairs using the strategies advanced in this book. Chairs may benefit, the department may change and develop, faculty may experience positive growth. As shown in Table 2, faculty may experience outcomes in relation to the chair's self-development, the chair acting as an academic leader, the interpersonal relations between chairs and faculty, and the processes used to bring about or address faculty issues. Chairs might ask themselves:

1. How does my own growth and development impact faculty?

2. How am I serving as a leader of faculty in the department?

3. How do I relate to faculty interpersonally?

4. How do my growth, leadership, and interpersonal skills impact the process I am using to bring about change in individual faculty and in the department?

Table 2
Faculty Outcomes

Chairs . . .	Faculty Members · · ·
*Role model a balance between personal and professional life. Take time out for leisure activities - realize that faculty will accept this time out as valid.	Learn how to create balance in their own lives. It is especially important for new faculty -- those under pressure to perform.
*Spend time learning about faculty interests, needs and aspirations.	Feel they are valued, being heard, being helped.
*Seek out other chairs and individuals on campus for insight into addressing faculty needs.	View assistance as positive. Create openness in the department where faculty can ask for assistance.
*Learn the strengths and weaknesses of senior administrators.	Experience a chair who can be an effective advocate with administration for their needs.

Table 2 continued

Chairs . . .	Faculty . . .
*Demonstrate academic vitality by remaining active in their fields.	See the chair as vital and interested in intellectual endeavors.
*Help build a focus for the department and keep it before the faculty.	Feel that they can contribute to the focus. They recognize what will be rewarded, what the institution values, and learn of sense of community.
*Spend time carefully building faculty ownership of ideas.	Feel they are heard, listened to. They support departmental concepts or ideas.
*Do not view change as immediate; rather, they view change as evolutionary, incremental.	Are not suddenly jolted out of their usual patterns. They feel that change is of their own making.
*Are aware of faculty needs for resources, information, and time off to pursue individual professional interests.	Feel supported. Welcome information and opportunities where they can regroup or pursue their favorite projects.
*Consciously build a faculty data system to respond to requests in a timely fashion.	May not acknowledge the need for this system; but understand the importance of information about conveying their accomplishments to others.
* Let faculty express their ideas freely, do not stifle ideas, and do not personalize criticism.	Are encouraged to trust and to be open with chairs and with other faculty in the department.
*Spend time listening to faculty in one-on-one situations.	Feel important, feel that needs will be heard even if they are not addressed.
*Help faculty set goals at the beginning of the year and review accomplishments of the goals with faculty at the end of the year.	Have an opportunity to talk about their professional careers with the chair, and discuss personal and professional needs; have an opportunity at the end of the year to reflect on progress.

Table 2 continued

Chairs · · ·	Faculty . . .
*Are willing to provide both positive and negative feedback to faculty about performance.	Hear about both strengths and areas for improvement.
*Actively advocate for faculty needs and interests with senior administrators on campus.	Feel that the chair is their "advocate" or "protector".
*Continually improve as scholars or teachers so they can be good role models and mentors for faculty.	Realize that the chair shares similar values; that the chair can provide assistance, even serve as a collaborator in teaching or research.
*Take time from a busy schedule to appreciate faculty, praise their work, and acknowledge their areas of strength.	Feel good about their job and about themselves.
*Adapt strategies to specific faculty needs.	Feel respected as individuals.
*View faculty assistance as a process, a series of steps that unfold in a linear or non-linear fashion.	Slowly work toward goals, begin making changes; do not make changes; hopefully do not regress.
*Realize that not all individuals are "open" to assistance; some people will not change.	Need to help themselves.
*Read through these recommendations, and actively work to incorporate them into their style.	Will hopefully become more satisfied, productive, motivated, departmentally and institutionally oriented, and feel good about their work.

Implementing the agenda

Consider starting an orientation program for chairpersons on your campus if one does not already exist. Individuals typically learn the role from practical experience, and veteran chairs have much to offer in the way of practical tips. Ask these veterans about the strategies they use to address difficult faculty problems.

Read books about human developmental needs so that you can recognize the needs of faculty in various stages of their careers. Granted, such reading may be outside your academic area, but the ideas may be useful as you work with faculty at different points in their academic life.

Read books on serving others and other-centered leadership. These skills are useful when working with faculty, self-sufficient professionals in their own right.

Write into your job description the responsibility to assist faculty in their professional growth so that you consciously allocate time for this activity. Chairs can be weighed down by numerous responsibilities related to evaluating faculty, preparing reports, and putting out fires. Consider faculty growth as an equally important responsibility.

Develop your own set of faculty-oriented goals. Identify the primary goals you have for helping faculty during the academic year. Share these goals with faculty during beginning-of-the-year or end-of-year reviews.

Attend workshops on interpersonal skills, especially those that review good consultative skills such as active listening, feedback, coping, and confrontation. Participate in activities where you can observe or listen to your approach through role playing, videotaping, or audio-recording.

Create a career plan for your own professional future. Identify five- and ten-year objectives. Share this plan with others whom you respect and ask for their feedback.

Renegotiate your own contract for effort and rewards with faculty so that they see you not only as a faculty "evaluator" but also as an individual who facilitates the careers of your faculty.

Recognize that some strategies take less time to carry out than others. Look at the "Topical Index to Strategies" in Appendix B at the end of this book.

Celebrate the job of establishing a positive department for faculty. Recognize that the "excellent" chairs in our project often found the growth and development of their faculty as a major satisfaction in their job.

REFERENCES

Andersen, K. J. "In Defense of Departments." In D.E. McHenry and Associates, *Academic Departments,* San Francisco: Jossey-Bass, 1977.

Baldwin, R. and Others. *Expanding Faculty Options: Career Development Projects at Colleges and Universities.* Washington, D.C.: American Association for Higher Education, 1981.

Baldwin, R. "Adult and Career Development: What Are the Implications for Faculty." In *Current Issues in Higher Education, 1979.* Washington D.C.: American Association for Higher Education, 1979.

Baldwin, R., and Blackburn, R. "The Academic Career as a Developmental Process." *Journal of Higher Education,* 1981, *52,* 598-614.

Barber, S.P. "Faculty Development Needs as a Function of Status in the Academic Guild." In *To Improve the Academy.* A Publication of the Professional and Organizational Development Network in Higher Education, 1987.

Bennis, W.G. "An O.D. Expert in the Cat Bird's Seat." *Journal of Higher Education,* 1973, *44,* 389-398.

Bennis, W.G., and Nanus, B. *Leaders: Their Strategies for Taking Charge,* New York: Harper & Row, 1985.

Bennett, J.B. *Managing the Academic Department.* New York: American Council on Education - Macmillan Publishing Company, 1983.

Black, A. *The Story of Bridges.* New York: Whittlesey House, 1936.

Boice, R. "Counseling Colleagues." *The Personnel and Guidance Journal,* 1982, *61,* 239-240.

Bolton, R. *People Skills: How to Assert Yourself, Listen to Others, and Resolve Conflicts.* New York: A Touchstone Book, Simon & Schuster, Inc., 1979.

Booth, D.B. *The Department Chair: Professional Development and Role Conflict.* AAHE-ERIC Higher Education Research Report 10, 1982. Washington D.C.: American Association for Higher Education, 1982.

Bowen, H., and Schuster, J.H. *American Professors: A National Resource Imperiled.* New York: Oxford University Press, 1986.

Boyer, E.L. *College: The Undergraduate Experience in America.* New York: Harper & Row, 1987.

Bragg, A.K. "The Socialization of Academic Department Heads: Past Patterns and Future Possibilities." A paper presented at the Annual Meeting of the Association for the Study of Higher Education, Washington, D.C., March 1981.

Brammer, L. *The Helping Relationship: Process and Skills.* (2nd ed.) Englewood Cliffs, New Jersey: Prentice-Hall, Inc., 1979.

Bridges, W. *Transitions: Making Sense of Life's Changes.* Reading, Mass: Addison-Wesley, 1980.

Brinko, K. T. "Instructional Consultation with Feedback in Higher Education," *Journal of Higher Education,* in press, 1988.

Brown, J. D. "Departmental and University Leadership." in D. E. McHenry and Associates, *Academic Departments,* San Francisco: Jossey-Bass, 1977.

Burke, D. "The Academic Marketplace in the 1980's: Appointment and Termination of Assistant Professors." *The Review of Higher Education,* 1987, *10*, 199-214.

Burley-Allen, M. *Listening: The Forgotten Skill.* New York: John Wiley and Sons, Inc., 1982.

Caplow, T., and McGee, R.J. *The Academic Marketplace.* Garden City, New York: Anchor Books, 1965.

"Carnegie Foundation's Classification of More than 3,300 Institutions of Higher Education." *Chronicle of Higher Education,* July 8, 1987, pp. 22-30.

Clark, S., and Lewis, D. *Faculty Vitality and Institutional Productivity.* New York: Teachers College, 1985.

Corcoran, M., and Clark, S.M. "Professional Socialization and Contemporary Career Attitudes of Three Faculty Generations." *Research in Higher Education,* 1984, *20*, 131-151.

Cornford, F.M. *Microcosmographia Academica: Being a Guide for the Young Academic Politician.* Chicago: University of Chicago Press, 1922.

Creswell, J.W. *Faculty Research Performance: Lessons from the Sciences and the Social Sciences.* ASHE/ERIC Higher Education Report No. 4. Washington D.C.: Association for the Study of Higher Education, 1985.

Dyson, F. *Disturbing the Universe.* New York: Harper & Row, Publishers, 1979.

Eble, K. *The Craft of Teaching.* San Francisco: Jossey-Bass, 1976.

Eble, K. "Chairpersons and Faculty Development." *The Department Advisor,* 1986, *1*, 1-5.

Fink, L.D. *The First Year of College Teaching.* New Directions for Teaching and Learning, no. 17. San Francisco: Jossey-Bass, 1984.

Fisher, R., and Ury, W. *Getting to Yes: Negotiating Agreement Without Giving In.* New York: Penguin Books, 1981.

Furniss, T. *Reshaping Faculty Careers.* Washington D.C.: American Council on Education, 1981.

Gilligan C. *In a Different Voice: Psychological Theory and Woman's Development.* Cambridge, MA: Harvard University Press, 1982.

Heider, J. *This Tao of Leadership: Leadership Strategies for a New Age.* New York: Bantam Books, 1985.

"Higher Education Reformers Take Up Challenge to Give Teaching- and Teachers - More Clout." *Chronicle of Higher Education,* March 16, 1988, p. 1.

Kanter, R.M. "Quality of Work Life and Work Behavior in Academia." *National Forum,* 1981, 35-39.

Kimberly, J. R., Miles, R. H. and Associates. *The Organizational Life Cycle*. San Francisco, CA: Jossey-Bass, 1981.

Kimble, G.A. *A Departmental Chairperson's Survival Manual*. New York: John Wiley & Sons, 1979.

Kirkpatrick, D. L. *How to Manage Change Effectively*. San Francisco: Jossey-Bass, 1985.

Kouzes, J.M., and Posner, B.Z. *The Leadership Challenge: How to Get Extraordinary Things Done in Organizations*. San Francisco: Jossey-Bass, 1988.

Kubler-Ross, E. *Death: The Final Stage of Growth*. Englewood Cliffs, New Jersey: Prentice-Hall, Inc., 1975.

Lazarus. B., and Tolpin, M. "Engaging Junior Faculty in Career Planning: Alternatives to the Exit Interview." In *Current Issues in Higher Education, 1979*. Washington D.C.: American Association for Higher Education, 1979.

Lewis, K. "Individual Consultation: Its Importance to Faculty Development Programs." In K. Lewis and J. Povlacs, *Face to Face: A Sourcebook of Individual Consultation Techniques for Faculty/Instructional Developers*. Stillwater, Oklahoma: New Forums Press, Inc., 1988.

Lewis. K., and Povlacs, J. *Face to Face: A Sourcebook of Individual Consultation Techniques for Faculty/Instructional Developers*. Stillwater, Oklahoma: New Forums Press, Inc., 1988.

Lowman, J. *Mastering the Techniques of Teaching*. San Francisco: Jossey-Bass, 1984.

Mager, R.F. and Pipe, P. *Analyzing Performance Problems*. Belmont, California: Fearon Pitman Publishers, Inc., 1970.

March, J.G. "How We Talk and How We Act: Administrative Theory and Administrative Life." The Seventh David D. Henry Lecture, University of Illinois at Urbana-Champaign, Urbana, Illinois, 1980.

Marchese, T. *The Search Committee Handbook: A Guide to Recruiting Administrators*. Washington D.C.: American Association for Higher Education, 1987.

Mathis, B.C. "Academic Careers and Adult Development: A Nexus for Research." In *Current Issues in Higher Education, 1979.* Washington D.C.: American Association for Higher Education, 1979.

McKeachie, W.T. *Teaching Tips: A Guidebook for the Beginning College Teacher.* Lexington, Massachusetts: D.C. Heath and Company, 1986.

Miller, R. *Evaluating Faculty for Promotion and Tenure.* San Francisco: Jossey-Bass, 1987.

Nelson, W. *Renewal of the Teacher Scholar.* Washington, D.C.: Association of American Colleges, 1981.

Noonan, J.F. (ed.). *Learning about Teaching.* New Directions for Teaching and Learning, no. 4. San Francisco: Jossey-Bass, 1980.

O'Hanlon, J., and Mortensen, L. "Making Teacher Evaluation Work," *Journal of Higher Education,* 1980, *51*, 664-672.

Peters, T.J., and Waterman, R.H. *In Search of Excellence: Lessons from America's Best-Run Companies.* New York: Harper & Row Publishers, 1982.

Povlacs, J. "The Teaching Analysis Program." In K. Lewis and J. Povlacs, *Face to Face: A Sourcebook of Individual Consultation Techniques for Faculty/Instructional Developers.* Stillwater, Oklahoma: New Forums Press, Inc., 1988.

Rogers, C. *On Becoming a Person.* Boston: Houghton Mifflin, 1961.

Scanlon, W.F. *Alcoholism and Drug Abuse in the Workplace: Employee Assistance Programs.* New York: Praeger Publishers, 1986.

Schein, E. *Career Dynamics: Matching Individual and Organizational Needs.* Reading, Mass: Addison-Wesley, 1978.

Seldin, P. *Changing Practices in Faculty Evaluation.* San Francisco: Jossey-Bass, 1984.

Seldin, P. *Successful Faculty Evaluation Programs.* New York: Coventry Press, 1980.

Smith, R., and Schwartz, F. "Improving Teaching by Reflecting on Practice." In J. Kurfiss, L. Hilsen, S. Kahn, M.D. Sorcinelli, and R. Tiberius (eds.), *To Improve the Academy:Resources for Student, Faculty, and Institutional Development.* Professional Organizational Development. Stillwater, Oklahoma: New Forums Press, 1988.

TIAA-CREF Research Dialogue. "Employee Assistance Programs in Educational Institutions." No. 16, February, 1988.

Taylor-Way, D. "Consultation with Video: Memory Management through Stimulated Recall." In K. Lewis and J. Povlacs (eds.), *Face to Face: A Sourcebook of Individual Consultation Techniques for Faculty/Instructional Developers.* Stillwater, Oklahoma: New Forums, Press, Inc., 1988.

Thoreson, R.W., and Hosakawa, E.P. *Employee Assistance Programs in Higher Education.* Springfield, Illinois: Charles C. Thomas, 1984.

Tucker, A. *Chairing the Academic Department: Leadership among Peers.* New York: American Council on Education - Macmillan Publishing Company, 1984.

Appendix A

The National Study

Strategies used by academic chairpersons in assisting faculty members to grow and develop professionally were examined in a three-year study begun in 1985. The research methodology was qualitative, with a semi-structured interview protocol and follow-up campus visits serving as the method for data collection. Sponsored by TIAA-CREF and supported financially by Lilly Endowment, Inc., this national project involved two hundred department chairs on seventy college and university campuses.

Chairpersons who served as subjects for our project represented a special sample. The individuals were nominated on their campuses by senior academic administrators and faculty development specialists (where the position existed) for excelling in the professional growth assistance they provided to faculty.[9] These "excellent" chairpersons demonstrated distinguished records for supporting faculty members. They possessed strong interpersonal skills, encouraged faculty to participate in developmental activities, held the respect of colleagues as academic leaders and scholars, and understood the mission, direction, priorities, and orientation of the institutions they served. Fourteen percent of the chairs participating in the project were female and 86 percent were male. Participating chairpersons represented diverse disciplines. They were social scientists (for example, economists, sociologists, psychologists, and anthropologists), natural scientists (for example, physicists, chemists, medical scientists, and geologists), humanists and artists (for example, theater directors, English and foreign language specialists, historians and visual artists), and professionals (for example, engineers, architects, and journalists).

---

[9] We used the following question: "Please nominate three to five chairpersons (or their equivalents) on your campus who excel in assisting faculty grow and develop professionally."

The seventy campuses on which the two hundred chairpersons were employed represented four of the major types of higher education institutions as classified by the Carnegie Foundation for the Advancement of Teaching: research universities, doctoral-granting institutions, comprehensive colleges and liberal arts schools. Two year campuses and specialized institutions were excluded.[10] Institutions were located in thirty-three states and included campuses along the Atlantic and Pacific coasts, in the South and the Midwest.

The schools represented public and private campuses, and included institutions with substantial enrollments of Native American, Black, Hispanic and female students. A few of the schools had negotiated collective bargaining agreements with their faculty members. Numbers of students enrolled ranged from approximately 600 to over 40,000 students.

We conducted forty-five-minute telephone interviews with the two hundred nominees and made eight campus visits interviewing the chairpersons, their faculty members, faculty development specialists, academic deans and other administrators, to follow up on the telephone interviews.

Seven interviewers were trained in data gathering techniques. The interviewers maintained an ongoing dialogue concerning the inter-rater consistency of data recording and coding procedures. Analysis of interview data proceeded inductively, with applicable coding schemes unfolding as we listened to and read interview records and entered data on the computer. Analyses were assisted by use of the Dbase III+ database and SPSS-X computer programs. The interviews, site visits, and consultation of related literature provided triangulation for the data base. In the analysis used in this book, special emphasis has been placed on data derived from interview protocol questions concerning specific incidents of chairs helping a single faculty member in the department and the strategies chairs would recommend to a new chairperson.

-----

[10] We used the identification system advanced by the Carnegie Foundation for the Advancement of Teaching in the July, 8, 1987 *Chronicle of Higher Education.*

Topical Index to Strategies

Short-term Strategies